Charles Frederick Holder

Along the Florida Reef

Charles Frederick Holder

Along the Florida Reef

ISBN/EAN: 9783337107048

Printed in Europe, USA, Canada, Australia, Japan

Cover: Foto ©ninafisch / pixelio.de

More available books at **www.hansebooks.com**

ALONG THE FLORIDA REEF

BY
CHARLES FREDERICK HOLDER, LL. D.
AUTHOR OF LIFE OF CHARLES DARWIN,
ELEMENTS OF ZOÖLOGY, THE IVORY KING, LIVING LIGHTS, ETC.

WITH MANY ILLUSTRATIONS

NEW YORK
D. APPLETON AND COMPANY
1899

PREFACE.

The adventures and incidents of the following story do not belong to the realm of fiction. They are the actual happenings in the daily life of several boys, one of whom, the author, resided for five or six years upon a small key of the great coral-reef that stretches away into the Gulf of Mexico from the Florida Peninsula. A portion of nearly every day was spent in floating over the coral gardens, for which the locality is famous, or in hunting or fishing for the strange animals which there found a home. The excursions were made, as described, under the guidance of a naturalist who, while a surgeon in the army and stationed at the post, was studying the corals and other animals of the reef, and who relied not a little upon the young naturalists and divers to collect the specimens in which he was interested, and which, at the request of Professors Agassiz and Baird, ultimately found their way into the Smithsonian Institution, the Museum of Comparative Zoölogy at Cambridge, and other institutions of science throughout the country. The recollections of these days—the swimming-trips along coral banks, exciting chases after turtle and shark, visits to the haunts of the sea-gull, dives to the home of the queen-conch in the deep lagoon—are still fresh in the author's memory, and it is hoped that some of the enthusiasm of the boy naturalists of the reef, in outdoor studies, may be imparted to the young readers of this volume.

For a few illustrations taken from Elements of Zoölogy, written by the author jointly with J. B. Holder, the undersigned is indebted to the American Book Company, publishers of that work.

C. F. H.

PASADENA, CAL., *July, 1892.*

CONTENTS.

CHAPTER I.
THE LAND OF THE DANCING CRANE 3

CHAPTER II.
IN THE CORAL COUNTRY 27

CHAPTER III.
ON THE OUTER REEF 49

CHAPTER IV.
A RACE WITH A WATERSPOUT 73

CHAPTER V.
THE BEATING OF THE JACKS 102

CHAPTER VI.
RIDING A SHARK 120

CHAPTER VII.
THE TALKING-FISH 132

CHAPTER VIII.
THE DISAPPEARING ISLAND 147

CHAPTER IX.
Tom and the man-of-war 164

CHAPTER X.
The mystery of East Key 183

CHAPTER XI.
The isle of birds 194

CHAPTER XII.
Catching a man-eater 217

CHAPTER XIII.
A turtle turn 232

CHAPTER XIV.
The pet-house 244

CHAPTER XV.
Hauling the seine 255

CHAPTER XVI.
The hurricane 267

LIST OF ILLUSTRATIONS.

	PAGE
"A large fish, like a monster bird, rose partly out of the water" . . . . *Frontispiece*	
Paublo	5
The *Antennarius marmoratus* and its floating nest formed of Gulf-weed	17
Anthea cereus.	21
Sea-anemone and its young	22
A jelly-fish	26
Fort Jefferson	29
An uninvited passenger	30
Inside Fort Jefferson	32
Green turtle	36
The "Conch boys" catching turtles	38
Hawksbill or shell turtle	43
A game of leap-frog	45
Astræa pallida	53
Multiplication of polyps by spontaneous fission . . .	54
Remoras clinging by their sucking-disk to the under part of a shark	58
Sea-fan, or gorgonia	64
Spider-crab	65
Edible crab	72
Porpita pacifica	79
Velella limbosa	80
Preparation	83

	PAGE
Perpetration	84
Frigate-bird	85
Cypræa moneta	86
Black echinus eating into a rock	88
Sea-cucumbers	89
Fierasfer and young	90
Branch coral	93
Sea-egg	101
Tellina radiata	105
Toad-fish	106
Diagram of the growth of a sea-squirt or ascidian	115
Tom went headlong over the bow	118
Meandrina cerebriformis	123
Marine cray-fish	124
An octopus running	126
Argonaut with the shell. Argonaut without the shell	129
Octopus punctatus	130
Pearly nautilus	131
The sea-porcupine	135
The porcupine as a balloon	136
Scallop	142
Shells of living foraminifera	143
Brittle star	144
Jelly-fish	145
The basket-fish	157
Sword-fish and saw-fish	159
The bill or gar-fish	160
The sea-horse	162
Flamingo and nest	174
Portuguese man-of-war	177
Parrot-fish	182
Common salt-water mussel. The dancing scallops	200
Oysters, showing different stages of growth	202
Ocypoda, a marine crab that lives on land	205
Gecarcinus rusticola, a land-crab	207
Marine hermit-crab	210
Frigate-bird	212
The decorator	215

LIST OF ILLUSTRATIONS.

	PAGE
The blue shark	219
The pet shark	227
Walking-stick	230
Craw-fish	233
The lophius	246
Meandrina convexa	247
Sea birds	249
Dana's astrangia	254
Decorating in captivity	259
Luminous fish of the deep sea	263
Horseshoe-crab in trouble	266

ALONG THE FLORIDA REEF.

CHAPTER I.

THE LAND OF THE DANCING CRANE.

Leaving Key West—The expedition—Catching a kingfish—The Marquesas—Graining a Tartar—In the wake of a big ray—The spoonbill—A small Sargasso sea—The nest of a fish—The floating coral—Animal flowers—The dancing cranes—A sea of fire—The games of animals.

"ALL aboard for the Tuguses!" shouted a jolly-faced colored man.

"All aboard!" echoed three youthful voices.

The hawsers were cast off, the jib run merrily up by willing hands, and the trim schooner *Tortugas* bore away down Key West Harbor, headed for Garden Key, the land's end of the great Florida reef—the key of the Gulf of Mexico.

The *Tortugas* was a Government schooner

yacht, commanded by Captain David Ellis, and carried the mail from Key West to the end of the reef, being the only regular means of communication. On this trip the passengers comprised Dr. Bassett, his son Tom, and Dick and Harry Edmonston, companions of the latter and sons of the commanding officer of the district. The doctor was an enthusiastic naturalist. His object in visiting the great reef was to study the corals and collect specimens of all the animals found here; and the boys were looking forward to exciting and novel experiences in aiding in the practical work of collecting in the months to follow.

The wind was fair, and the *Tortugas* was soon bowling along with a mass of foam under her bow, starting the flying-fishes, and even attracting the attention of the sleeping pelicans that floated in the water here and there. By the docks and wharves of the Spanish-American town they rushed, passing Fort Taylor, with its frowning guns, then bearing away by the Sand Key light and heading, as the captain said, for "sundown."

"What you young gemmen like fo' supper?" asked Paublo, the cook, as the boys passed the galley. "Grunt, hogfish, grouper, snapper, conch, green turtle?"

"I'll take kingfish," said Dick.

"So will I," said Tom.

Paublo.

"Dat's always de way," rejoined Paublo; "de only fish I ain't got. But I kin cotch one; dish yer's a great place fo' kingfish," added the obliging cook, taking out a stout line from a locker and fastening a bright silvery sardine to the hook; "an' if one of you young gemmen will hold de line I'll git de fryin'-pan scotched."

"I'll hold it," said Harry, taking the line from the jolly Paublo, who went off to the galley, singing softly:

> "Ham fat, ham fat,
>   Frying in de pan,
> Ham fat, ham fat,
>   Cotch him if you can.
> Oh! git you in de kitchen
>   As quick as ebber can,

Hoochie koochie koochie,
I'm de ham-fat man."

Harry seated himself on the rail, line in hand, watching the last receding cocoanut trees of Key West. He had almost forgotten the kingfish, when a mighty jerk nearly pulled him overboard.

"I've got him!" he cried. But that looked doubtful, as the fish gave a powerful surge, taking the line through his fingers at a rate that made them burn. Captain Ellis luffed the schooner, and they shortly had the kingfish alongside. It proved to be a fine specimen, about three feet long, of a steel-blue and silver color, with a long and rakish jaw.

"Don' lift him by de line," cried Paublo, who came running from the galley, unshipping on the way a pair of grains which hung in the shrouds, "or you'll tear out his jaw. Now, hold him up."

Harry and Tom raised the fish slightly, while Paublo hurled the barbs into its neck; and by the combined efforts of the three the fish was lifted to the deck, where it thrashed around and gave them all a lively few moments, dodging its tail. Paublo now took it in hand, and before long a rich odor floated aft that told of a coming dinner and a good one.

Other kingfish were caught during the afternoon, the ground proving, as Paublo had said, one of the best. When the boys had wearied of hauling in big fish they joined the doctor, who told them something about Garden Key— their destination and home for months to come, and, as it turned out for the doctor and Tom, a residence of six or seven years.

"In 1818," he began, "Florida belonged to Spain; but in the following year it was purchased by our Government for five million dollars. This was considered a large sum at the time, but at present, with its valuable fisheries on the reef, the orange-grove industry of the main-land. the harbors and resorts, it is seen to have been very cheap; in fact, Key West alone could not be purchased for that sum.

"Having obtained the new possession, our Government found it necessary to fortify it; so in 1847 the central island of the Tortugas group was selected, and Fort Jefferson begun. There was an old-fashioned light-house there, as well as a cottage, which is mentioned in one of Cooper's novels. Previous to this time the island had been the resort of buccaneers and outlaws from all lands, who were finally driven away by the ships of our West India squadron.

"The islands are called Tortugas, which means in Spanish 'turtle,' because they have always been famous as the breeding-grounds of the green and loggerhead turtles. They are called keys, which is a corruption of the Spanish *cayo*, an inlet. Some call the group the Dry Tortugas, as there are no springs there, all the drinking water being caught in cisterns. Tortugas is sixty miles from Key West, and between the islands is the Marquesas."

"Will it be possible for us to stop over at the Keys?" asked the doctor of the captain, who stood near.

"I think so, sir," was the reply. "The way things look we shall just about reach there and be caught in a dead calm."

The captain's prophecy came true. The

wind gradually died away; the booms creaked and slashed to and fro as the schooner rolled in the ground swell; the reefing points beat a merry tattoo on the listless sails, and at sundown the Gulf, as far as the boys could see, was a sea of glass, the sun going down amid splendors they had never dreamed of.

Paublo took a belaying-pin and began tapping on the foremast, advising the boys to whistle for the wind; and Captain Ellis assured them that these two methods never failed in his experience to raise the wind if kept up long enough—a truism which was appreciated later on.

But, despite the shrill calls and the tattoo on the foremast, the surface of the Gulf remained as smooth as a mirror; and finally even Paublo became discouraged and brought out his violin, whiling away the time with song and dance. Finally, with the stars and the Southern Cross gleaming brightly, the party turned in, to awake the next morning and see over the rail a group of islands resting like gulls upon the water.

"We managed to reach here in the night,"

said Captain Ellis, joining them; "and as there is no wind you may as well go ashore."

The boys were only too delighted, and after a hurried breakfast the little dinghy was lowered away, and they were soon pulling up the blue channel that skirted the Key. The Keys were picturesque islands, with white, sandy beaches, covered with a mass of low bay-cedars.

When nearly opposite a little bay, some curious fins were seen cutting the water.

"Sharks!" exclaimed Dick, looking over his shoulder.

"I think so," replied Tom, wisely.

"Don't make any noise, boys!" whispered Dick, as he made a long lead or sounding-line fast to the thwarts, then with grains in hand stood prepared for action, as the boat neared the mysterious fins.

"Here's one coming this way," he added, raising the pole as he spoke. Hardly had he uttered the words when a great black body appeared near the bow and he let drive, with a result that almost appalled them. A large fish, in appearance like a monster bird, rose partly out of the water, coming down with a crash that sounded like the blast of a small cannon. The waves rocked the boat violently, and the occupants were thrown down in a body by the sudden shock. Tom had been holding the coil of rope, but had fortunately remembered to throw it overboard, leaving the end fast to the bow.

"That's not a shark!" said Dick, as he picked himself up from the bottom of the boat.

"I should say not," retorted Harry; "but what do you suppose it is? Just see it go!"

The fish was rushing away, making the water foam and boil.

"Stand by the line," shouted Tom, "it will be taut in a second!"

"Away we go!" cried Dick.

And go they did. For now the fish had taken the whole length of line and, with a sudden jerk, on rushed the dinghy, bow under, at race-horse speed.

"Cut the rope!" shouted Dick, excitedly, picking himself up for the third time. "He'll capsize us."

"Hold on a minute," said Tom, who had

caught the line at the notch; "I've got the hatchet, and when I'm sure he's too much for us I'll cut the rope."

But just then they heard Paublo calling to them from the schooner, between his rounded hands and at the top of his voice:

"Cut de line! cut de line! don't let him foul de line. It's a devil-fish!"

The boat tore along the channel at a rapid rate, but as it turned a curve the excited boys saw that their strange steed was rushing to its own destruction, for the channel ended in a mud flat.

They were right. In its terror the great fish ran up on the dead coral in about one foot of water. The line slackened all at once, and the boys now put out their oars and, after stopping the boat's headway, pulled off to watch the dying fish that was beating the water furiously. Its head was fully exposed, and, as they pulled in range, Dick put a load of buckshot into it and ended its struggles.

When, shortly after, the doctor and Paublo were brought ashore, and they all walked round to view their capture, Paublo said: "I thought it was a devil-fish; but it's pretty near it—one of de biggest rays I ever see. Sometimes dey cotch 'em here fifteen foot across, an' dey git foul with anchors an' tow smacks about in a mighty mystrus fashion."

"Are you joking?" asked Harry doubtingly.

"No," said the doctor, answering for Paublo. "I know of a case myself where a *manta* fouled the anchor of a good-sized schooner and towed it for a mile before it cleared. The fish has two curious projections," he continued, "which are sometimes called claspers; these occasionally are fouled with cables, and the fish rushes away in blind terror, towing the vessel, much to the astonishment of the sailors. Several cases have been known on the reef."

The boys carried away the tail as a souvenir, and then pulled around to the sandy beach off which the schooner was anchored.

"Give way hard!" said Paublo, who had the stroke oar, and with a rush the boat was sent on the beach, whereupon the boys all tumbled out and hauled her above the water-line.

They started at once to explore the beach, and soon came upon an old wreck, which the tides had evidently driven higher and higher, year after year, until it was now high and dry, the haunt of crabs and gulls, which had evidently taken complete possession. Tom noted one bird of so brilliant a red that he determined to secure it. A shot from his gun brought it down with a broken wing. It started for the water at once, but Tom dashed into the surf and caught it just in time.

"Isn't it a splendid fellow to set up in our collection?" asked Tom enthusiastically. "It's a spoonbill, isn't it?"

"Yes," the doctor replied, "and a fine specimen, too. Its feathers, you see, are blood-red, and its bill is spread out at the end, not unlike the bowl of a spoon. Hence its name, the roseate spoonbill."

After a stroll, followed by a rest on the beach, the party took to the boat again, intending to make a circuit of the little island. As they pushed out, Harry said, looking down through the clear water:

"The bottom of the sea is as beautiful as a garden."

"Yes," rejoined the doctor; "the corals, fans, plumes, and sea-weeds are the plants; the Gulf Stream moves through their branches as wind plays through the trees on land; and as land plants absorb the excess of carbonic gas, these marine forms secrete the lime salts, rejecting the soluble salts of sodium and other substances that are not necessary for them. The land plants purify the air so that we can breathe it, and the animal-gardens do a similar work in the ocean, purifying the sea-water, keeping down the excess of salts that would be unwholesome for the fishes and other animals."

"And how about the animal life, doctor?" inquired Dick.

"The likeness holds good," replied the doctor, "for there are many curious similarities. The seals, manatees, and whales are the cows of the sea; the sharks are the eagles; the crabs are the insects; the bird-of-paradise finds a worthy imitator in the fantastic angel-fish which we shall see among these very coral reefs. For every animal on land there is in the sea some creature which seems to fulfill the same office, though, of course, under changed conditions."

The conversation was here interrupted by the dinghy coming to a sudden standstill. It had run into a great bunch of sea-weed.

"It's a regular Sargasso sea," said Tom, laughing. "We could almost use this as an anchor."

"That has been done with some species," answered his father. "There is found near Tierra del Fuego a gigantic sea-weed called *Macrocystis pyrifera*, which grows in water two hundred and forty feet deep, and is so firmly rooted that vessels during smooth water are frequently made fast to it."

Here Dick, who had been towing after him a mass of the weed, suddenly noticed that some spherical pieces of the weed had been separated from the rest. Seizing one of them, he tossed it into the boat.

"Here's a marine base-ball," said he.

"This is a very interesting find, Richard," said the doctor, picking it up. "Your marine

The *Antennarius marmoratus* and its floating nest, formed of Gulf-weed. Fish natural size, the nest reduced.

base-ball is really the nest of a peculiar fish, about four inches long, which lives on the surface of the water in this gulf-weed. The nest is made up, as you see, of pieces of sargassum, wound in and out, and matted together in a curious fashion, and then held in its spherical shape by bands of a glutinous secretion from the fish that look like strings of jelly."

When the nest had been opened, the eggs of the fish were found fastened to the leaves in great numbers; and Dick, who still retained some of the loose pieces, was fortunate enough to find the odd fish itself.

"It is the *Antennarius*," said the doctor; "and a more curious fellow could scarcely be imagined. You will notice that he mimics the color of the sea-weed."

"And see," added Dick, "these things that look like bits of the weed on its head and fins are really part of its flesh."

The doctor had placed the prize in a pail of water, and, continuing, said: "They are slow swimmers, you see," as the fish moved lazily about, "and prefer to lie undisturbed among the protecting branches of the seaweed."

"I should like to see the baby fish when they are hatched," said Harry; "there must be a thousand of them."

"More than that," replied the doctor. "If all the eggs of fishes were hatched, or if all the young grew up, there would not be water enough on the earth to float them. There is always a fish of some kind that preys upon each particular species, and they in turn are devoured by others. There must, therefore, be many born, if any are to survive. But, without this check to the increase, the fish would multiply with marvelous rapidity. Suppose, for instance, the egg of the cod, which lays—by trustworthy calculations—over nine millions of eggs, should all be hatched and grow to maturity, the bodies of the cod alone would, before many years, seriously impede navigation."

The boys concluded that it was fortunate so many fish enjoyed a cod-fish diet.

The boat had now nearly completed the round of the island when, on making a sudden turn, they came upon a number of white cranes and gannets. The cranes rose quickly, but Tom, the sportsman, who usually had his gun ready, brought one down, very neatly, on the wing. The stupid gannets had not moved even yet, and Tom declared that they well deserved the name of "boobies." The boys pulled out and picked up the body of the crane. It was a beautiful white bird, with a yellow patch on its breast.

"It is a heron," said the doctor; "and this yellow spot on its breast is supposed by some observers to be capable of giving out a bright phosphorescence in the dark."

"Don't shoot!" said Harry, as Tom took aim at the gannets, who were still regarding their strange visitors in stupid amazement. "Let me start them."

Taking a large piece of coral which he had picked up on the beach, he threw it toward the birds. The gannets rose slowly, as the coral splashed up the water, but, to the great astonishment of the boys, the coral, instead of sinking, floated lightly on the water like a piece of wood.

"All stones don't sink," said the doctor, laughing to see Harry's look of surprise. "That coral doesn't mean to be left out of our collection; seriously, I think we had better keep the specimen," he added; and the floating coral was again picked up.

"But what is it—and why is it—doctor?" asked Harry.

"It is what might be called the skeleton of the coral called *Meandrina spongiosa*," explained the doctor; "and when the animals die it becomes bleached. It is very porous, and the pores being full of air, the coral floats easily on the water."

Anthea cereus (Opelet).

"Hold on a minute," said Dick, as the boat grated over some branch-coral, knocking off thousands of tips. The dinghy was stopped, and Dick, leaning over the side, tore off a branch of dead coral. Hanging to it was a beautiful anemone. Dick handed it to the doctor, who placed it in a glass of water.

Very soon the anemone threw out its beautiful tentacles, which were like the petals of a flower.

"It is more like a flower than an animal," remarked Harry.

"Yes," said the doctor, "and related to the corals. You can form a very good idea of the coral animals from this anemone, which differs from the coral polyp mainly in the fact that it does not secrete lime. They all belong to the class *Actinozoa*. The body, as you see, is a cylinder, its top fringed with tentacles, and directly below is the stomach, hanging in the body, and held in place by vertical partitions. Water in this animal seems to serve the purpose of blood."

Sea-anemone and its young.

"*His* blood is no 'thicker than water,' then?" said Tom, with an air of sober inquiry.

The doctor laughed and resumed: "The tentacles, under the microscope, are seen to be covered with minute cells, in each of which is coiled a delicate, hair-like javelin that is darted out on the slightest provocation. Now, if a small crab or shrimp bumps against these tentacles, myriads of these darts shoot out, striking and paralyzing the intruder, while the tentacles draw it down into the stomach of the anemone."

"Have they no eyes?" asked Tom.

"Yes, they are here at the base of the tentacles, but are too small to be seen in this little specimen. The anemones are produced in several ways, as from eggs, and by what is called budding. The latter process is extremely simple, the animal apparently tearing off bits of its disk as it moves along, each of which in a few days throws out tentacles and becomes a new anemone."

The mast of the *Tortugas* could now be seen beyond the beach. Paublo, who had been searching for turtles' eggs, hailed the dinghy, and soon after they were alongside. An awning was rigged over the stern, tempering the heat so that it was not too great for comfort.

While lying around on deck, the attention of

the boys was attracted by the actions of a flock of cranes. One by one they had collected until eight or ten stood on the sand. Their movements were decidedly curious. Now some of them would rush around, hop in the air, rise just above the surface, and dance along in a dandified fashion, pecking at imaginary objects, and uttering strange cries that provoked no little merriment among the boys.

"This must be the land of the dancing crane," said Harry.

"It looks very much like it," replied the doctor, "and is just as truly dancing as the motions of men and women. Many birds have this habit, but the cranes are the most remarkable. The cock of the rock, a South American bird, is also a dancer. The other birds form in a circle about it, and when it retires exhausted another bird takes its place."

As Captain Ellis had predicted, the wind went down with the sun, and the water became as smooth as glass, reflecting the countless stars, and gleaming with phosphorescent light. The schooner appeared to be resting in a sea of molten metal, and wherever a fish leaped from the water a blaze of seeming fire appeared.

"Take some of the water up," said the doctor to Dick, who was dashing an oar into the water to see the great waves of light that followed, handing him a tall glass for examining delicate specimens.

Dick reached down and filled it with the gleaming liquid. Upon examination, they saw the cause of the phosphorescence. Innumerable minute animals threw out the light, like so many electric lamps. The doctor pronounced them *Noctilucæ*, while little crustaceans in the water undoubtedly added to the illumination. Introducing a stick and whirling it about, Dick took out his watch and could almost make out the time by the living light—an experiment which was successfully carried out upon another occasion.

"It's freshening up," said Captain Ellis, coming forward and pointing to a slight ruffle on the water, "and I propose we get under way."

The boys jumped to the halyards with the sailors, and very soon the *Tortugas* was moving quietly away, leaving the islands of the dancing crane far in the distance.

A jelly-fish.

CHAPTER II.

IN THE CORAL COUNTRY.

Garden Key and the Dry Tortugas—Bob Rand and Long John—A pet pelican—A large fort—Getting settled—Home on a coral key—Riding the green turtle—The aquarium—Angel-fish—Surgeon-fish—Leap-frog with a fish—Long John's pets—The fishing and collecting tools, coral hooks, and grains.

WHEN the boys awoke next morning and staggered on deck, they found the *Tortugas* bowling along with a fair wind, a big square sail out to help her along, and a strange dinghy towing astern, while sitting on the weather rail were two men, evidently the owners, who had just come aboard. They were introduced as Long John and Bob Rand to the boys, who unanimously agreed that they were very singular characters.

The new-comers were pilots, wreckers, and fishermen. Long John, as his name indicated, was remarkably tall, over six feet, and very thin, with the reddest face imaginable, set off by a head of very spare gray or yellow hair. Bob Rand was short and stout, with a face, if it were possible, even redder than John's.

The men greeted the boys cordially. Long John was very talkative, while Bob Rand would take off his glazed hat, scratch his head, and prepare to speak, when Long John would answer for him. As this happened on almost every occasion when Long John was present, Bob rarely entered into the conversation. But the boys found him a good friend and agreeable companion in the long months that followed, both men being with them almost constantly.

The morning was perfect. To the starboard and north a large key was seen, apparently hanging in the water. This was East Key, while beyond it Middle and Sand Keys appeared like bits of silver against the blue of the Gulf. Dead ahead was Bush Key; beyond rose the grim walls of a great fortress, while still farther away, seemingly from out a long line of mist, rose the tall tower of Loggerhead Light-house.

Fort Jefferson

All around the group, and far to the south, stretched a line of foam that seemed to indicate impassable reefs.

Gradually the walls of the fortress came more plainly into view; the boys could distinguish the waves as they beat upon the coral shores, and, running past Sand Key, the *Tortugas* suddenly wore around and headed up the narrow channel that led to the east of the fort.

At a word from the captain the crew manned the halyards and jib downhaul, the schooner was luffed, and as she came up, away went the anchor, the mainsail came rattling down, and the *Tortugas* lay snugly moored under the frowning walls of Fort Jefferson, on Garden Key, or the Tuguses, as Paublo preferred to call it.

Long John and Bob Rand shoved off to bring the luggage-boat, and as they rowed away in the dinghy the boys were surprised to see a pelican, that had been quietly flying overhead, suddenly circle down and try

An uninvited passenger.

to alight on Long John's head, flapping its great wings and uttering a queer asthmatic sound.

John pushed the bird away, and then it tried

to alight on Bob Rand, but failing in this, it settled down in the dinghy, as if determined to have a ride, whether welcomed or not.

"Well, that's the queerest thing I ever saw," said Tom, laughing. "Are all the birds around here as tame as that, Paublo?"

"Not all, sir," replied Paublo. "Dat's one o' John's pets. It follows him all over, jest like a dog; an' w'en he's too lazy to fish fo' bait de old pelican does it fo' him. Dey's a queer pair. Long John kin tame anything."

Bob Rand was soon seen sculling back a large flat-bottomed boat, into which the luggage was thrown; and after its return the boys eagerly scrambled in, quickly reaching the shore, finding themselves under the shadow of one of the largest forts in the world. There was no time to examine their surroundings, as their luggage, the boxes, and cans had to be taken into the fort. Paublo, with the aid of some colored boys, soon had everything loaded upon wheelbarrows, and with the young naturalists on either side to superintend the work, the march was taken up the long broad walk, over the drawbridge, and into the big fort.

The doctor was assigned quarters in a small brick cottage on the west side, and here the party speedily made themselves at home. Knapsacks were emptied, boxes unpacked, the alcohol was poured into numerous small cans; books and drawing implements, microscopes, and other apparatus were placed in order on a large table in an adjoining room, after which the expedition was, as Dick said, "ready for business." The weather was delightful; the mellow moonlight streamed through the open window, and from the distant reef came the sullen roar of the surf, above which was heard occasionally the cry of a laughing gull.

Inside Fort Jefferson.

Next day the great fort was thoroughly explored. The boys wandered through the groves of cocoa palms and bay cedar that gave Garden Key its name, paced the cedar avenue that led up to headquarters, and even played a game of base-ball on the pleasant parade-ground, turfed with Bermuda and a thick wiry grass.

Their island home comprised thirteen acres, most of which was covered by the fort, then being erected by the Engineer Department of the United States. The fort, one of the largest of its kind in America, was built of brick, was half a mile around, with three tiers of guns, and surrounded by a moat eight or ten feet deep, the only entrance being the sally-port, through which the boys had passed; even this could be closed by a heavy drawbridge, making the grim fortress completely inaccessible.

The island was made up of ground coral, shell, and the hard portions of a lime-secreting sea-weed, and was so low that it would have been washed away time and time again by the hurricanes had not, as Tom said, the fort and its sea-wall held it down.

Their home was a portion of a growing atoll on the very western end of the reef and the center of the Tortugas group. The little harbor was perfectly protected, affording safe facilities for boating and sailing inside the reef, and was famed as a zoölogical collecting ground. Acres and acres of coral reef stretched away in every direction, bathed by the warm waters of the Gulf Stream, that swept by and through the olive-hued coral branches, burdened with food from the warm belt and the Caribbean Sea.

That night the doctor told the boys about the reef, and outlined their plans. "We must," he said, "combine business with pleasure. We are going to make a complete examination of the reef, and collect every animal upon it—the various kinds of shells and corals, the birds, fishes, and sea-weed. And, further, we must learn all about the ways and habits of the inhabitants of this wonderful garden of the sea, observe how the coral grows and how fast; in fact, store up all the facts we can. A portion of every day we will spend on the reef; then at night we can assort our finds and discuss them."

It is needless to say that the boys looked forward to this programme with delight and pleasant anticipation.

The doctor had made some arrangement by

which Long John and Bob Rand were to aid them with their sloop from time to time, while an old sailor, named Busby, and a Seminole Indian, called Chief, became in time companions on many of their trips.

Paublo had been induced to undertake the culinary department; the commodore, as Busby was termed, fell into the dignity of boat-keeper, and in a very short time the little party was settled and ready for work.

The first experience of the boys on the key was an exciting one. They were busily at work unpacking when a lusty shout from Paublo called them out.

"If any of yo' young gemmen wants to go turtle-ridin'," he said, "I'm goin'."

No further invitation was necessary, and the boys followed him down through the sally-port, to the quarters, and finally out around the sea-wall. The moat here was about one hundred feet wide, half a mile around, and eight or ten feet deep, the bottom being a clear white sand, so that every object was visible, and the boys soon made out a number of dark forms lying on the bottom.

"Dey's green turtle," whispered Paublo, in reply to Dick's question, "and don't make any noise or dey'll start off."

Green turtle (*Chelonia viridis*).

"But how are we to catch them?" asked Tom.

"Why, dive fo' 'em," replied Paublo; "yo' want to swim along right up behind, an' w'en yo' git on top dive down, sudden-like, an' grab de turtle right back of de neck, an' jest hang on; don' let go. Dat's de secret—don' let go."

The boys threw off their clothes and, lowering themselves into the water, slowly swam toward the turtles, Paublo standing on the sea-wall instructing them by various mysterious motions.

Tom reached a turtle before the others, and dived, according to instructions, and opening his eyes under water had no difficulty in approaching the sleeping animal. How big it looked, with its broad back and extended flippers! Tom almost hesitated, wondering what he should do if it turned on him. But there was not much time to think, so he reached out and grasped the turtle firmly by the shell just over the head. The turtle opened its bleary eyes, and, with a convulsive rush of terror, reached the surface for breath, then dashed away, dragging Tom as if he was being towed behind a steam launch.

"Hold on!" shouted Paublo, running along the wall. "Hold on tight!"

By this time Harry had appeared, Dick's steed having become alarmed and given him the slip.

"Hold on" was good advice, Tom thought, but difficult to carry out. The turtle, crazed with fear, was beating the water with its powerful flippers, endeavoring to dislodge its rider under water. Now Tom's head would disappear, then it would come up with a rush, and

The "Conch boys" catching turtles.

the vigorous puffing of boy and turtle would strike the air together.

"Lay out sideways!" again shouted Paublo, which Tom did and found much easier.

Up the moat he went, passing Harry, who was having a hard struggle, shouting, laughing, choking, all in one breath, and converting the hitherto smooth waters of the moat into a whirl of foam. The end of the inclosure reached, the turtles whirled about and dashed back again.

Such an exciting sport the boys had never experienced—a race on turtle-back—and the walls of the fort echoed back shouts of laughter and cries that brought out the doctor, who heartily enjoyed the sight from one of the port-holes of the fort.

Even turtles will become tired, and these were no exception; after making the run several times they gradually relaxed their exertions, and the boys, by putting their knees upon the shell and raising themselves up, presented a greater surface, and finally stopped the huge animals against the wall.

Paublo, who had been the general and suggester of the various movements in the capture, now entered the water and fastened a rope about Tom's turtle, and with the aid of the rest soon had the big reptile upon the wall and in the barrow, when it was wheeled away to be converted into savory steaks later on.

"I suppose that's our fresh beef," said Harry as he put on his clothes.

"All you'll git here, sah," replied Paublo as he rolled the barrow along.

"Talk about lassoing wild horses," said Tom to his father, who had joined them, "it's nothing to riding turtles."

"It looked as though it might be fun," said Dick dolefully.

"It will be your turn next time, Dick," said the doctor; "you will have plenty of riding."

"Yes," added Paublo, who was glad to get rid of this part of the work, "we'll kill turtle two times a week all summer, an' den dere's de cotchin' an' turnin' moonlight nights on Loggerhead an' East Key. Dere's heaps o' fun in dat."

On their way back the boys found the doctor, who had gone ahead, in possession of a little house on the edge of the channel by the wharf. It was built on dead coral rock, and out from it into the water extended an inclosure of the same, with a smooth concrete walk on top. The basin so formed was a natural aquarium, and having been stocked from time to time by Long John and Chief, had now been handed over to the naturalist as an experimental station.

As they came up, the party found Long John sitting on an upturned barrel, with a knife in one hand and a piece of conch in the other, from which he was shaving pieces and tossing them to a motley crowd of fishes that scurried to the surface. The fish were so tame that they almost jumped out of the water in their efforts to reach the bait.

The fish were new to the boys, and most interesting, owing to the great variety of shapes and colors.

"Isn't that an angel-fish?" asked Tom, as in and out among John's queer pets darted a fish of gorgeous hues. Slashes of blue, gold, brown, and white covered its body, while the long dorsal and ventral fins gave the marine dandy a most fantastic appearance, not unlike that of a gayly dressed harlequin.

"Yes, that is an angel-fish," replied his father, "and the species are well named, I think, for they are the most beautiful of all fishes."

Long John here stooped down and put his hands into the water, with fingers spread apart. Three or four little fishes at once swam between his fingers, rubbing their gills against them in the most friendly manner. On the surface floated several gar-fish, their long, delicate noses armed with sharp teeth; parrot-fish, with real bills; cow-fish, with horns; snappers, porgies, toad-fish, and numerous others, all crowding each other and fighting for the white bits of conch meat tossed in to them by Long John.

"There's one fish that don't get anything," said Dick, "and see how he acts when the others come near. He looks just as though he was trying to hit them with his tail."

"That's exactly what he is doing," said Long John, "and every time. He doesn't belong here, but he comes in every day. Just hand me that net, and I'll show you what he does."

Tom handed him the scoop-net, and Long John, dexterously inserting it beneath the fish, landed him on the wall. It looked much like a common porgie, but when Long John, telling the boys to watch, touched the fish with his knife, to their surprise a sharp, knife-life weapon darted out of a sheath near the fish's tail, and was as suddenly sheathed again.

"Gracious! it's a regular knife, isn't it?" exclaimed Dick, with wide-open eyes.

"You'd think so, if you should feel it," said Long John. "Every fish that comes within range thinks so, too, for this wicked little chap gives 'em a slash, just as you saw him doing when he flung his tail round."

"It is called the *Acantharus chirurgus*, which may be translated surgeon-fish," said the

Hawksbill or shell turtle (*Caretta imbricata*).

doctor, as he touched the fish again, and the ugly-looking knife was thrust forth.

"I reckon if he knew he had such a handle as that to his name he'd be so mad he'd kill every fish in the place," said Long John, with a chuckle, as he threw the vicious fellow back.

Other fish swam in mid-water—delicate jelly-fishes coming to the surface now and then with a graceful sweep of their waving tentacles, several small green turtles, and here and there a good-sized hawk's-bill or tortoise-shell turtle, the kind furnishing the shell from which combs and other articles are made.

"Keep still!" whispered Long John, with warning finger. "Keep still, and you'll see a game of leap-frog."

And, surely enough, they did, but the "frogs" were a turtle and the fish. The hawk's-bill was floating with its back several inches out of water, when suddenly a gar-fish leaped completely over it. Another made the attempt, half turning in the air; two more followed suit —one turning a somersault—while still another, not quite so dexterous, failed in his act of lofty tumbling, and landed plump on the turtle's back, startling it so that it dived out of sight.

IN THE CORAL COUNTRY.

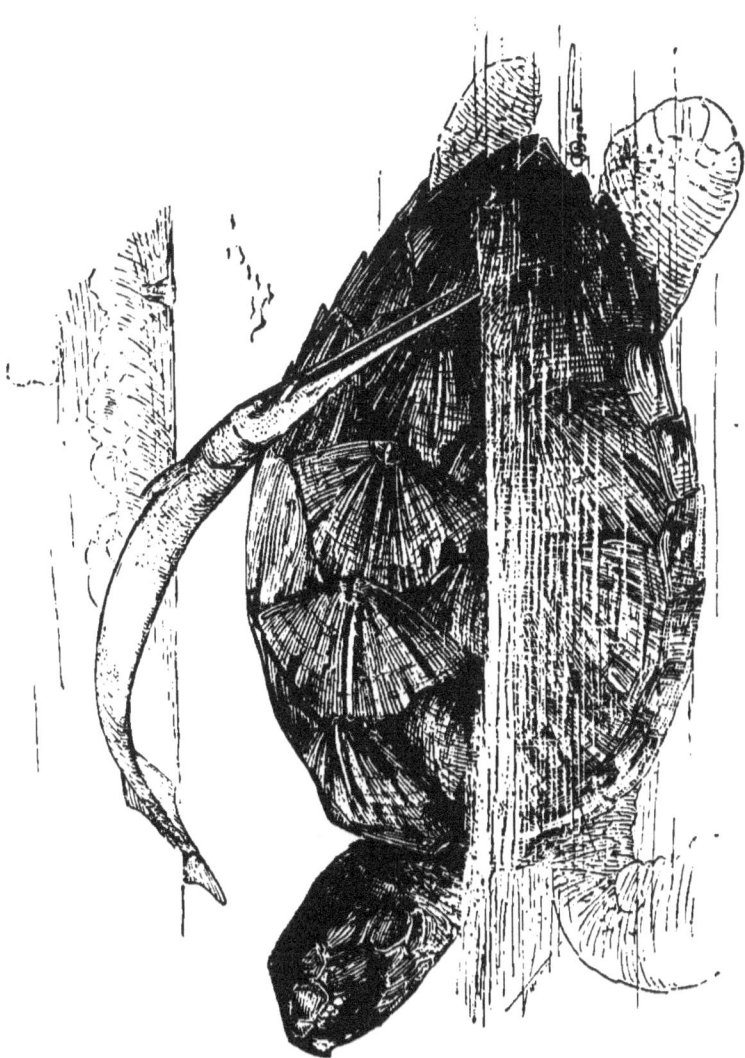

A game of leap-frog.

"I didn't know that fishes played games before," remarked Harry.

"They do, though," replied Long John; "and, as for these fellows, they give that poor turtle no peace. The minute he comes to the surface they begin their tricks, and if they can't jump over him they find some floating stick or straw and practice on that. Oh, fishes are much the same as you boys, I tell you—full of fun and all kinds of nonsense."

"All these animals seem to know you," said Harry.

"I reckon they do," was the reply. "I kind of look at 'em as belonging to me."

"Doesn't Bob Rand care anything about them?" asked Dick.

"No," replied the long fisherman. "Bob's got a sojer-crab, and that's all he cares for. I reckon you'll find it in the shanty," motioning with his knife over his shoulder.

The boys entered the office, and, after looking about for some moments, espied a singular object—nothing less than a common clay stemless pipe on the floor, slowly moving along.

"A haunted pipe!" cried Dick, laughing.

"Haunted by a hermit crab," retorted Tom.

And this was Bob Rand's pet, as from the bowl projected the deep purple and red claws of a soldier or hermit crab, that had taken possession of the pipe-bowl, and roamed about the office at will. It did not require much persuasion on the part of the boys to obtain this curious pet from the obliging Bob, and Diogenes, as he was christened, became then and there a conspicuous object in the household.

Paublo, after killing the turtle, had spent the morning fitting out a boat for use on the reef, and now came up to report that it was in readiness, whereupon the entire party started for the middle wharf, where both the *Rosetta* and the dinghy awaited them. In the former had been placed two large cans containing diluted alcohol for the reception of specimens. A number of long coral-hooks (iron instruments or tongs not unlike small oyster-claws) and three or four pairs of "grains"—long poles ending in two-tined spear-heads, with barbed points—some fastened to the poles, others fitted on with a socket and held by a cord, were arranged in the boats; and over the bows were hung several scarp-nets. A jug called a "monkey," used for carrying water, with the oars and a sprit-sail, completed the outfit of the *Rosetta;* while the dinghy carried the small seine and cast-net, and also provided room for the overflow of passengers.

Dinner was quickly over, and then, as the doctor called out, "All aboard for the reef!" a rush was made to the wharf, and in high spirits the young naturalists were speedily under way, pulling with rapid strokes across the deep, blue water toward the outer reef.

CHAPTER III.

ON THE OUTER REEF.

Wonders of the ocean garden—The angel-fish—Living sponges—Cigars afloat—The growth of a coral key—The shark and sting-ray—Gigantic coral heads—The remora—The malthea—Living sleeve-buttons—Drifting over the reef—The box-crab—The black squall—Making the five-foot—A narrow escape.

THE sun rose upon a glorious day. There was not a cloud in the sky; the water was as smooth as glass, save where the flapping tail of some big fish splashed the surface. The subdued roar on the outer reef sounded like far-off music, the white keys and the azure of the bright sky were reflected again and again in the water, the whole scene seeming to the boys a dream of enchantment.

Old Busby led the way in the dinghy, with

Tom, while the doctor and the rest of the expedition, with Long John, followed in the *Rosetta*. Before long they left the channel, and came suddenly upon the reef, which here rose almost perpendicularly from the channel and bristled with innumerable points of coral. Deep down among the green moss-fronds an anemone, looking much like the weird passion-flower, turned its fair face toward them; angel-fish dashed by, their gay bands and wing-like fins resplendent with color; gayly striped morays darted in and out of the shadows of the sea-fans and feathers, and the gorgonias, brilliant with rainbow-tints, were surrounded by duller-hued conchs and hermit crabs, sea-eggs, and devil-fish.

"Isn't it wonderful!" exclaimed Tom. And indeed it was. In a moment they had passed from the blue water to a veritable garden of coral spread over acres of reef; in shoal water and deep; on hill-side and plain; in forest-like groups and garden-like beds, in clusters, in circles, in hedges; domes like the round-topped mosque of the Orient; sponge forms that mocked the Turkish minaret; Laplandish huts and the

Gothic minster; cups, vases, and the classic urns; antlers of deer, of moose, of elk; flowers, vines, brakes, and mosses—all these forms came before them as they drifted slowly along and looked down upon this vast ocean garden.

As Tom hurled his spear at a small parrot-fish, which darted under the boat, the weapon landed in a large black mass about three feet in diameter and concave on top, like a huge vase.

"Hallo, what's this?" he cried, hauling away at the mass.

"It is a sponge," his father replied. "The color represents the living part."

"Why, are sponges animals, doctor?" asked Harry from the other boat.

"Naturalists admit them to the ranks of animal life, though, of course, among the very lowest forms," the doctor explained. "If you examine them closely in the water, you may see a slight current over the pores and openings, which shows that the necessary nourishment is thus absorbed while it circulates through these cavities. The common sponges, as we use them, are but the skeletons."

The boats were now gradually nearing Bush Key, with its scraggy trees, when Dick exclaimed:

"Why, there's a cigar in the water!"

"So it is," said Harry, nearly tumbling overboard in an attempt to reach it.

"Sold again!" laughed Tom, who had secured one; "it's only a stick."

"You'd find them hard to smoke, boys," said the doctor. "They are more useful than all the cigars that could be sent over here from Havana. They are the seeds of the mangrove tree, that you see over on Bush Key. The reef of the State of Florida has been formed mainly by the corals and the mangroves."

"Tell us how, doctor," said Harry, who was always ready for information.

"Suppose," said the doctor, "this clear water on which we are drifting should be visited by a single egg of the star-shaped coral called the *Astræa*. It settles on a bit of shell. In a few days some tentacles spring out, and the tiny polyp seems only a solitary sea-anemone. Then a little growth of lime, secreted by the anemone, forms on the shell, and soon overspreads it with a jagged coating. Then another polyp grows

Astræa pallida (living).

beside this one, perhaps by division or budding, and the single egg that first drifted here has become two. This goes on indefinitely, until the bottom all around is covered with coral-rock. Then, when these polyps decay and die, the sea-sand sifts in; other corals grow on this; floating matter is caught and added to the growing reef; forms of branching corals appear, together with gorgonias, or sea-fans and feathers; all these are eaten or crushed down by great worms and coral-eating animals. Upon this decay still other forms of coral grow; shell-fish of various kinds make it their home; delicate corals that need protection from the waves grow up in the lagoon formed within the shallow circle; as the reef becomes higher, sea-weeds and corallines are added; every particle of refuse adds to the up-building of this curious island; and now, just as the dry layers, or top-dressings, appear above the waves, along comes Dick's 'cigar.' The larger end of the mangrove seed strikes the sand or mud collected on the reef, the waves drive it still farther on, and, touching the soil, it sends out little shoots. These soon obtain a foothold, and

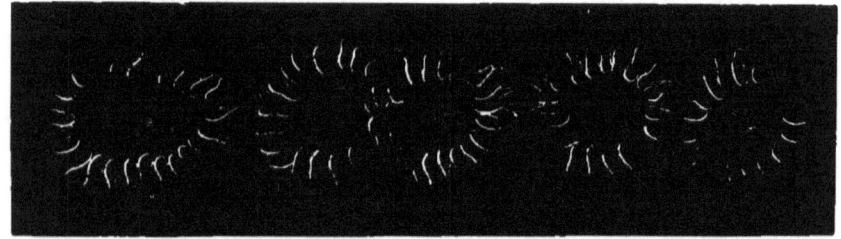

Multiplication of polyps by spontaneous fission.

thus a mangrove tree is started. These being self-propagating by shoots and rootlets, a growth in time may extend around a whole island. Other waste matter of the sea is accumulated, the influence of winds and tides changes the surface, and Nature furnishes suitable plants to flourish in the new soil which the decay of vegetable and animal organizations is continually increasing and enriching. That is the secret of reef-building, Bush Key being an example in this group of the aid which the mangrove gives."

While the doctor had been talking, the boats had slowly drifted toward the key, when right ahead a large sting-ray leaped from the water, flapping its wing-like fins in the air a moment, then coming down with a crash that was heard all over the lagoon. A large fin showed itself above the water, rushing after the ray toward a shoal near the key.

"It's a shark chasing a sting-ray!" shouted the old boatswain from the bow of the dinghy. "Give way, lads, give way!"

The boat surged ahead in the direction of the great fishes. The shark was gaining on its less rapid victim, and the ray repeatedly leaped into air to escape the rushes the shark made at it. Suddenly the ray took a desperate chance as it neared the shoal, and, instead of turning, dashed upon it; the flat body passed through the scant eight inches of water with a rush, and in an instant it was through the breakers and in the blue waters of the Gulf. The shark, following in blind haste, could not force its big body over the shoal, and was soon high on the reef. The boat's crew were quickly upon it, but, on account of the shark's tremendous efforts to free itself, they dared not touch it. In its struggles the fish would bend nearly double, and then, suddenly straightening out, would hurl the water over the boys, who had now left the boat and were wading about in the shoal water, dodging the shark's tail and trying to get within striking distance. Finally, Tom hurled his grains into the shark's head. This only increased the creature's struggles, but Busby, wading up to the writhing monster, struck it a terrific blow, breaking its backbone.

"It's easy enough, when you know how," he said, laughing.

They were all soon at work, cutting up their prize.

"Stand still, Tom," said the doctor, presently, as he lifted the shark's jaw and held it so that it easily fitted over Tom's head.

"Eight rows of teeth!" said Dick, counting

them. "What a time the young sharks must have when cutting their teeth!"

"Yes," said Harry, feeling of the terrible weapons, "and each one is saw-like and sharp as a knife."

"All the teeth except the front row lie flat," explained the doctor, "when not in use. As you see, they move up and down; but when the shark was after the ray I feel sure they were all vertical and ready for action."

For his share of the prize the boatswain took the liver, intending to try out the oil.

"Sharks are not entirely worthless animals, you see, after all," said the doctor. "The teeth are used by many savage islanders for weapons, the liver is taken out for the oil it contains, and in the East the tails and fins are valuable articles of commerce, while the skin, as with us, is used for various purposes."

"What do you call this shark that we have caught, doctor?" asked Harry.

"It is a shovel-nosed shark," he replied. "There are at least a hundred different species of sharks now known to naturalists, and this gentleman had an enormous forefather, away back in what is called the Tertiary period. That ancestor must have been a hundred feet long, with teeth as large as your open palm."

"What is this?" interrupted Tom, striking at a black body hanging to the shark, just under water, which Long John now exposed to view by turning the body over.

"Take it by the head and pull it off," said

Remoras clinging by their sucking-disk to the under part of a shark.
(*Adapted from Brehm.*)

the boatswain; "it won't hurt you; it's only a sucker."

But this was by no means easy, for the curious object clung so fast that only by a violent wrench could Dick and Tom tear it from the shark.

"It is a remora, and a very interesting fish," said the doctor. "It follows the larger fishes and attaches itself to them by this disk, refusing to leave them even when they are dead, as you see."

"That's why we call 'em 'suckers,'" put in Busby.

"They are sometimes called 'ship-stayers,'" continued the doctor, "and one of them is said to have changed the history of the world and given the Roman Empire to Augustus Cæsar."

Doubly interested by so historic and important a fish, the boys gathered around this curious specimen and examined it minutely.

The disk, which was the principal object of curiosity about the remora, was oval in shape, and on the very top of the head. It resembled in construction a Venetian blind, for it was composed of what the doctor called "oblique transverse cartilaginous plates," and Dick said were "slats of gristle." These were supplied with delicate teeth or hooks that helped it to cling.

"But how did it help Augustus Cæsar?" inquired Harry.

"There is a legendary story that one of these fellows fastened itself on Antony's galley at the great naval battle of Actium, and thus allowed the galley of Augustus to obtain the advantage in the onset," the doctor explained. "Hence its name—the 'ship-stayer.'"

"I have heard you can catch turtles with 'em," said Busby, "although I've never seen it done."

"I have heard the same thing," rejoined the doctor. "In Mozambique the natives, it is said, keep this fish in a tub of water, and then, when a turtle is sighted, the remora, with a cord tied to its tail, is tossed overboard. Instinctively it fastens itself to the unconscious turtle, which is speedily hauled in by the fisherman."

"Well, well, a live fish-hook; that's an idea!" laughed Tom. "Let's keep it and try. Only it would be rather rough on us if Mr. Remora should fasten himself to a shark instead of a turtle."

"What's that smoke on Bush Key?" asked Dick, pointing to the island, a short distance off, from which a column of smoke was rising.

"Hardly a volcano, Dick," replied the doctor. "I believe it is a signal that our lunch is ready. Long John thought we would like some coffee after grubbing, as he called it, in the water; so he took the dinghy and the lunch Pablo prepared for us, and I imagine is now waiting for us."

"Well, I'm ready," said Dick; and Harry and Tom answered by jumping into the *Rosetta*. The others followed suit, and in a short time they were on Bush Key, where they found Long John frying mullets, having spread a cloth and the lunch on the white sand. The boat was pulled up high and dry, and soon the boys were doing justice to the mullets which Long John had caught in his cast-net a few minutes before.

"I've seen the time," said the fisherman, as he sat down at the invitation of the doctor, "that we wouldn't care to sit here. The big hurricane in '50 made a clean sweep of it. I believe there was one tree left; but you could have sculled the dinghy over the key."

"You don't have hurricanes often, do you?" asked Harry.

"Not very," replied the fisherman; "onc't or twic't in ten year or so. But when they do come," he added, "they wake snakes; wipe out everything. That one cleaned out Long Key; you'd never know 'twas there."

The lunch over, the boys investigated a pelican's nest—a big bunch of drift-wood—in one of the low trees, while the two boatmen repacked the hampers. Soon after they shoved off, and began again the circuit of the great reef.

Wading along, the party continued their investigations in tide-water; and Dick and Harry, coming upon a large piece of coral, which had been worn almost through, rolled it over. In doing this they disclosed a natural pool beneath the coral, and at the bottom lay a most peculiar fish.

"Well, here's a curious fellow, doctor," cried

Dick; "what under the sun—or rather under the coral—is it?"

The doctor stooped down and examined it. "You are right, Dick; this *is* a curious fellow, indeed!" he said. "The fish is called the *Malthœa*. It has, as you see, no fins for swimming, but is provided with short feet, like paddles, with which it moves over the muddy bottom in which it lives."

"He's lazy enough," said Dick, as the fish, even when touched, showed but small desire to move.

"It is one of the sluggish fishes," continued the doctor, "of which there are a number. This one, you will notice, is formed and colored so as to appear like an inanimate substance—a part of the sea-bottom. But here is a singular thing. Do you see here, right over the mouth, a sort of depression or pit, from the roof of which hangs a curiously colored pendant?"

The boys, after a careful look, saw it distinctly.

"Well," said the doctor, "that is the means by which the *Malthœa* makes up for its sluggishness. The broad mouth rests on the mud; above it this curious-looking pendant twists and writhes, and looks so much like a tempting and luscious worm to the hungry prawn or inquisitive crab that, if the living bait is approached too closely, the great mouth yawns wide open, and good-by to Mr. Crab or Mr. Prawn!"

"Well," said Tom, "we've seen a living fish-hook and a living bait; if we keep a sharp lookout, perhaps we shall find a live reel or fishing-pole!"

Sea-fan, or gorgonia.

"Here's a curious shell," cried Harry, who had waded out into deeper water, lifting up a gorgonia a foot in diameter, and of a rich yellow hue. Clinging to it were a number of beautiful oblong shells of about the same tint—tending toward pink.

"Those are fan-shells," said their guide, "and are parasites on the gorgonia, or sea-fan. They make beautiful sleeve-buttons."

The boys supplied themselves with a stock of these natural cuff-buttons; and then Harry,

Spider-Crab.

turning over a rock that was alive with spider-crabs, pulled a beautiful blue one out of the water and tossed it to Long John, to be placed in the water-pail for security.

"Here's an odd fellow," Tom called out a moment after, stooping over the rock and bringing up a curious-looking spider-crab.

"That is a deep-water one," said the doctor; "some of his big relatives, measuring nearly three feet across, have been hauled up in the South Atlantic from a depth of nearly two miles."

"As deep as that?" exclaimed Harry; "why, I should think the pressure was too great for animals to live at such great depths."

"Water is practically incompressible," explained the doctor; "that is to say, it can not be forced into a smaller compass, as solids can. So, as all these creatures are filled with water, the pressure is equalized. If you lower an empty bottle two miles under water it will often remain intact, and yet the pressure in deep water is simply tremendous. A deep-water crab, for instance, must withstand a pressure, at such depths as two and a half miles, of a number of tons—as against the fifteen pounds' pressure which a fish at the surface experiences. But all animals are adapted for their particular sphere in life."

Noticing a bubbling in the sand, Dick thrust his hand under and forced up what the doctor declared to be a box-crab; as he demonstrated, it had the faculty of closing its legs around its body in such a manner as to seem a solid piece. When released, it opened out and showed its curious make-up—a round body, covered with queer brown spots and ridges, even the claws being formed in grotesque shapes.

"You'll find lots of them crabs on the reef," said Busby, who was passing.

"Hallo, look over yonder!" came a sudden shout from Long John. "We've got to clear out of this, and be quick about it, too!"

They all followed the direction of his warning gesture, and saw on the horizon a small black cloud, its lines as distinct as if drawn with a brush. As they sprang into the boats and pulled for Long Key the cloud seemed to increase, and so rapidly did it gain upon them that in ten minutes from the time they sighted it the cloud was almost on them. Landing hurriedly, they hauled the boats on shore, and, turning the dinghy keel up, they crawled beneath it; and just in time. With a darkness that turned day into night, and a low, far-away moaning, that grew into a roar, wind, rain, and sand burst upon them in a hurricane, with a fierceness that threatened to carry away the boats. The wind howled and shrieked, the lightning flashes lighted up the scene in fitful glances, while the sea was beaten into clouds of foam, lifted into the air, and hurled far beyond them over the island.

"It won't last but a minute," shouted Long John from somewhere; and even as he spoke it began to grow lighter; the rain ceased, and they crawled from beneath the boat. The cloud or squall disappeared almost as rapidly as it came, and in twenty minutes from the time the storm arose the sun was shining again from a clear sky.

A start was now made for home. The squall had left a stiff breeze behind it, and with sails hoisted on the *Rosetta*, and towing the dinghy astern, they were soon rushing toward Garden Key, gunwale under.

"Well, that was a blow!" said Tom.

"Oh, it's nothing when you get used to it," said Long John. "I've seen seven or eight squalls movin' around, lookin' jest as if they were painted on the sky. It's quick come, quick go, with 'em; but, if you keep your weather eye open, you know how to steer clear of 'em."

"This is not the way home, is it?" asked Dick, as Long John headed the flying boat between Long and Bush Keys.

"It's one way," the latter replied, trimming the sail still more.

Crossing the reef, the boat dashed into blue water and bore away to the south, where the long line of breakers seemed to form an impassable barrier. Long John kept along the reef until nearly opposite the sally-port of Fort Jefferson, which could just be seen a mile away, then suddenly he bore off before the wind, and headed straight for the breakers.

The boys looked at the raging surf in some anxiety, and then glanced at Long John. He was cool and calm, as was also the old boatswain, Busby.

"I suppose he knows what he's about," whispered Harry to Dick.

"Slack off the fore-sheet!" shouted Long John quickly, standing up now and scanning the distant fort.

The commodore did as directed, and the boat bent over and rushed headlong toward the reef, seemingly to destruction.

"I don't care to swim in that surf," said Harry, looking uneasily at the mass of foam they were rapidly approaching.

"You won't have to swim," answered Long John, who had overheard him, "if you hang on tight."

It was too late to object, so they all drew a long breath and "hung on tight," as advised. With a mighty rush the boat plunged into the breakers; now on top of one, again nearly buried under another, careening over so that the boys sprang to the windward, then luffing and sliding close by one almost bare head of coral to avoid another; covered with foam and spray, drenched from head to foot, and almost before they could catch their breath, they were over the reef, safe and sound, and tearing along in the smooth water of the inner reef.

The boys were amazed. "What kind of navigation do you call that?" asked Tom, wiping the spray from his eyes; while the doctor said: "Why, John, you cleared those heads only by about six inches."

"That's all the room there was, sir," replied Long John with a grin. "It's a regular channel," he added; "we call it the 'five-foot.' I've been through when it was worse."

"But how did you know how to steer?" asked Harry.

"Well," said Long John, "if you'll promise not to let on, I'll tell you. Keep down the reef until the Garden Key light is just on a line with the third chimney of that big brick building of the fort; then let her drive, and, if you can keep her head on, you're all right."

"And if you can't?" interrupted Harry.

"Well, sir," was the reply, "it's one of the things it wouldn't pay to miss—it's a bad place for sharks."

While talking they had neared the lower

part of Long Key, where they stopped to put their corals in the barrels that Long John had previously provided for the purpose, as in this way, he explained, coral was prepared. The shells which they had found were also placed in stagnant water, or buried, this being the only way to thoroughly clean them, while many other finds were dropped into alcohol for future study.

Having disposed of their specimens, they shoved off again, and were shortly in their quarters, tired out, but well pleased with their first day on the reef.

Edible Crab.

CHAPTER IV.

A RACE WITH A WATERSPOUT.

The boatswain's home—After the norther—Long Key—Miles of spirulas—A shell with a dye—The water-spout—The gull and pelican—A live cowry—Pierced by the black echini—The dweller in a sea cucumber—Wonders of the five-foot channel—A worm with a door and hinge—The old wreck—A young sea serpent—Pegging a turtle.

COMMODORE BUSBY, as the boys sometimes called the old boatman, and as, indeed, he styled himself, was inclined to be a martinet. He was a great stickler for etiquette, and in the seventeen-foot *Rosetta* would, if allowed, have divided all hands into port and starboard watches, installed the doctor as admiral, with Tom as captain of the fleet. When the *Rosetta* went about, Busby generally sat amidships, tending the fore-sheet, and his "Ready about, sir! Hard a lee, sir! Haul it is, sir!" were all delivered with a precision that would have done credit to a fifty-gun frigate.

The commodore took great pride in the *Rosetta*, which the doctor had decorated. She was painted a rich vermilion outside, white within, her seats cushioned, and the guards and bulkhead ornamented with attractive pictures from the doctor's brush. Tin cans had been inserted beneath the decks, so that she was a life-boat as well as a picture of beauty. Busby did not fancy her name, *Rosetta*, and after a race in which Tom sailed her to victory in half a gale, and brought her in half full of water, he rechristened her the *Roaring Gimlet*, as being characteristic of her method of boring through the waves under a press of canvas.

The commodore had quarters in a large rambling building outside of the fort, where, in one end, he had a room fixed up, from which led a little balcony. From here he could see a weather-vane, set by the compass, on the top of the building, and here, according to his own account, he took "dead loads of comfort." The doctor gave him a flag and rigged him a flagstaff, and every night and morning the rheumatic old sailor would be seen hoisting and lowering the national emblem. From a hook in his room hung an old spy-glass—a remarkable instrument made from several others, and from which the commodore pretended to discern not only various wrecks and sails, but traces of storms and foul weather.

One morning, a week or two later, the boys were visiting the old man. They were sitting on the little balcony, looking off on the smooth water, and listening to the cries of the laughing-gulls, when Busby unhooked his wonderful spy-glass and peered through it for a few seconds; then looking steadily over the top a moment, he announced that it was going to blow, and blow hard, and that things had better be made snug. The boys wondered how he knew, and each taking the glass in turn tried to peer through it, but could see nothing but a blur. They could learn nothing further from the old boatswain, who, taking down his flag, hobbled down the stairs of the big building and was soon at the boat-house, hoisting the *Rosetta*, or the *Roaring Gimlet*, as he preferred to call her, out of the water.

Busby was a true prophet, as before many hours it began to blow, and by night a heavy gale broke upon the key. The cocoa-nut trees in the fort were lashed and torn, and as far as the eye could see was a mass of boiling foam, while the water rose so high that the boys sailed about on planks in the interior of the fort. This weather continued for three days before the "norther," as this wind is called, was succeeded by a dead calm. Then the boats were put in readiness for a trip, and it was decided to start at Long Key and follow along the entire length of the reef, which was now piled with dead coral, weeds, and deep-sea shells tossed up by the waves. Long Key was appropriately named, being a long, attenuated island, half a mile in length and from twenty to fifty feet wide, running north and south, just across the channel from Garden Key, and so near that the boys often swam to it.

The key was entirely destitute of trees, a little grass constituting its flora, while its sole inhabitants were hermit and other crabs. At the north end it was joined to Bush Key by a partly submerged flat, and here, on an apology for an island, grew several mangroves that gave shelter to various pelican nests.*

The party was soon ashore at Long Key, selecting many beautiful specimens from the numberless richly colored weeds and shells strewed along the sand. The univalves, or one-shelled specimens, were the most numerous, but upon the pieces of gorgonia many delicate bivalves of exquisite red and blue tints were found.

The severity of the storm was evident in the numbers of strange objects piled upon the beach. A narrow white band, extending almost as far as the eye could see, was found to be composed almost wholly of the shells of the little *Spirula*, one of the most beautiful and delicate of the cephalopods. It was a perfect spiral, divided like the nautilus into chambers, with pearly par-

---

* Since the time of my residence here Long and Bush Keys have been almost entirely obliterated by a hurricane.—AUTHOR.

titions; but, strange to say, the shell, like the cuttle bone of other species, was concealed in the body and only found after the death of the little squid, when the air-chambers caused it to rise to the surface and it was washed ashore. Though diligent search was made at various times, the boys were never able to secure one alive. They are probably extremely delicate creatures, and were killed by the waves and torn from the shell before being cast upon the beach.

The rich shells of the marine snail *Ianthina* were almost as frequent, the animal in many cases being intact. On the water their appearance was extremely beautiful, the rich purple coloring, in various shades and tints, standing out in strong contrast against the white fairy-like raft of bubbles by which they are kept upon the surface. By pressing the animal, the boys found that the rich purple ink would stream out over their fingers.

"This ink would make a good dye," said Tom; "I'm going to put some on my handkerchief and see how long it will stand."

"It will last several years," answered his father; "and some think it the ancient dye of the Tyrians."

Among these animal wrecks were found numbers of the *Porpita* and *Velella*, their shin-

Porpita pacifica.

ing skeletons looking like dismantled hulks. The color of the *Porpita*, in those spread before them, was a rich purple, but where the animals had died and the skeletons lay bleaching in the sun, it presented a structure that in delicacy could be compared only to spun glass. The

Velella was even more beautiful, the body part somewhat resembling the *Porpita*, except that it had a curious sail-like membrane that would

Velella limbosa.

readily catch the breeze. On other occasions the boys often watched fleets of these charming ships sailing over the blue waters in company with the Portuguese man-of-war.

These objects, which in the North were valued as rare specimens, were banked up in windrows by the storm, with fishes, shells, sea-fans, and gorgonias, in which the boys literally burrowed, gradually moving up the narrow key.

The doctor and Harry had gained on the others, and had become so completely absorbed in the treasures before them that they were utterly oblivious to their surroundings. They had almost reached an old fishing schooner that had been hauled up, when they heard a shout, and, looking back, saw a very unusual spectacle. Tom and Dick, who had lingered behind, were now rushing along the beach as if for their lives, while, not a hundred yards behind them, running parallel with the key, towered a huge waterspout, its top lost in the clouds. With gigantic curve it came surging on, hissing like a steam-engine, and tearing up the shallow bottom at a terrible rate. A race with a water-spout is not a pleasant pastime. It ran so close upon them that its drippings were like a heavy rain. Thus far they had kept even with it, but it now surged ahead, and, changing its direction, headed for the old schooner on the key. Tom and Dick were safe, but Harry and the doctor appeared to be in danger.*

---

* I ran with this spout for several hundred yards, and had difficulty in keeping apace with it. The noise was like that made by a

"Run for the spout and get behind it," shouted Long John, who had come in and was hauling his boat off shore.

The doctor and Harry ran past the spout, which was now very near the shore, and, when out of harm's way, turned to watch the monster's progress. On it went, boiling and hissing, in the direction of the fort, passing down the face of the north wall, a sublime and magnificent spectacle.

"That was a close shave!" said Harry; and the others fully agreed with him.

The line of march was again taken up, and before long they reached the head of the island, where a narrow strait separated Long Key from Bush Key. While stopping to overhaul a pile of sea-weed their attention was attracted by the comical asthmatic cries for food made by some young pelicans from their nests of drift-wood in the mangrove trees near by. The old birds were hard at work, diving for fish in the lagoon.

---

steam-engine. Examination later showed that the spout had plowed a trench in the reef two or three feet deep. Small fishes were killed, and flocks of gulls followed in the wake.—AUTHOR.

The boys watched one, which was near them, with no little curiosity. It would flutter an instant over its prey, then plunge down, and with

Preparation.

open, dip-net bill resting on the water, would adjust the catch in the capacious pouch beneath. In one of these expeditions a gull, with trained and eager eye, hovering near, settled down upon the pelican's broad head, and as the fish was tossed about, preparatory to swallowing it, the

Perpetration.

thievish gull adroitly snapped it up and sailed away with a derisive "Ha, ha!" while the pelican, as if accustomed to this sort of pocket-picking, simply flapped heavily up again to renew its search for food. But the gull, as was speedily seen, had laughed all too soon; for down upon it from the neighboring shore swooped a strong-winged man-of-war hawk, or frigate-bird.

Frigate-bird.

With a shrill cry of alarm the gull darted now this way and now that, in zigzag lines, striving with all its power to escape. Fear and fatigue prevailing, he let his choice stolen morsel slip from his grasp; then the man-of-war bird, with a lower swoop, clutched the falling fish and bore it away to the nearest rock.

"So the struggle for existence goes on," said the doctor; and, turning from hawks and gulls, the party continued their search for specimens.

The doctor made the first find of interest. Turning over a submerged piece of dead coral, several brown egg-shaped creatures appeared, covered with curious short tentacles. They were evidently mollusks; but where was the shell?

"Now watch the transformation," said the doctor, as the boys crowded around; and, touching one of the animals, the curious covering rapidly drew in from beneath, exposing the exquisitely polished shell of a *Cypræa* or cowry, the micramock of the reefers.

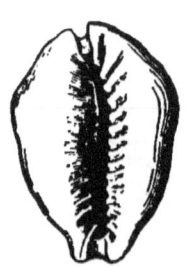 

Cyprœa moneta.

"I have often wondered," said Harry, "how they retained their polish; this explains it."

"Yes," replied the doctor. "They live in these rough places, and to protect the shell, and rebuild it when worn away or broken, this singular covering is thrown out. You are all familiar with the spotted cowry; it is a relative of this; the family is a very large one. The *Cypræa moneta,* or money cowry, is imported from the Maldive Islands in great numbers, and sent to the African coast, where they are taken as money. About three thousand of them are equal to fifty cents; so when you go there have your pockets made large. The orange cowry is another valuable species, and is used to distinguish the chiefs of the Friendly Islands."

The party now left Bush Key, and were wading over the submerged fringing reef that separated the lagoon from the deep waters beyond, Long John poling the *Rosetta* along, on the lookout for craw-fish near them, and occasionally coming in to receive some specimen too large to carry. As Tom attempted to pick up a big black echinus, or sea-urchin, he uttered an exclamation of pain, some of the needle-like spines having pierced his unwary fingers.

"They belong to the star-fish family," the doctor explained, as Tom nursed the wounded hand. "There is another of the same branch," pointing to a large worm-like animal coiled in a pool.

"Take it, Dick; one is enough for me. I won't be selfish!" said Tom dryly.

Black echinus eating into a rock.

Dick, with Tom's discomfiture in mind, poked it cautiously with his foot, and finally picked it up. It looked like a large caterpillar, covered with wrinkles, and armed on the under side with an array of queer, short tentacles.

Sea-cucumbers (trepang).

"It is the trepang—a holothurian," said the doctor, in answer to Dick's "What in the world is it?"—"and a regular article of diet with the Chinese."

"Hallo, see here!" cried Harry, as the trepang, which he had taken from Dick's unwilling grasp, suddenly doubled up, and from its open mouth shot out a slender stream of water; "is it a fish fire-engine, or a living squirt-gun? And look at that!" he exclaimed excitedly, as out of the trepang a queer fish-like head appeared, followed by an eel-like body, white and ghostly.

Harry dropped the fish in some trepidation. "Good gracious!" he cried, "what is it?"

But the doctor quickly picked up this strange visitor and placed it in a glass of water in the boat.

"It is a messmate-fish—the *Fierasfer*," he explained—"one of the boarders of the trepang."

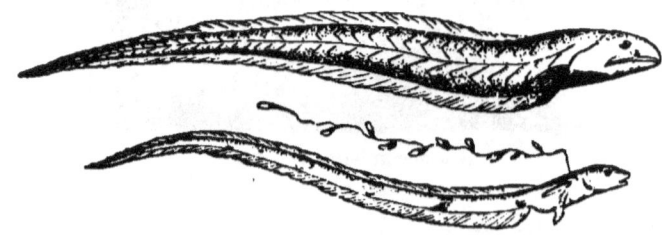

Fierasfer and young.

The curious animal was a perfectly formed five-inch fish, so transparent that its internal organs could be seen; but evidently out of its element, for, even as the doctor spoke, it gave a few struggles in the water, sank to the bottom, and soon died.

Many of the large holothurians were found to contain these ghostly boarders, but in no instance did they live after being taken from their living home.*

As the boys wandered along the reef they unexpectedly came to the five-foot channel, through which Long John had so skillfully steered them. The water being too deep to ford, they all boarded the *Rosetta*, intending to cross to the other side and continue the tramp; but the beauty of the coral and gorgonias in the channel caused them to linger. On its confines was a perfect forest of coral—tree coral, it is called, on account of its great size. From the gunwale of the boat the swaying tops of the forest were in full view, the millions of delicate flower-like polyps of the coral in full expansion upon the branches. The least touch or jar would send every one of these flower-like

---

* The naturalists of the Naples Aquarium have observed the *Fierasfer* leave its host and return, the latter being made tail first; the action of the trepang in taking in water evidently aiding in the accomplishment of the return.

animal mouths instantly out of sight, within the structure which constitutes its cell. The coral tree reminded them of the bare trunk and branches of a veritable tree denuded of its leaves. The brown film or membrane covering the whole was, the doctor said, the connecting tunic that held and united the community. "*E pluribus unum*," he said, "is their motto, and how many in one we may imagine when we note the individual blocks that lie upon the reef, or even one of the single trees of this forest beneath us."

As they looked down into the clear water they noticed that some of the tips of the branches were white, and denuded of the soft, brown covering or mantle, and soon discovered the cause. Lying across the top branches was a great caterpillar-like worm, longer than one's hand. As Tom introduced his hook under it, and slowly lifted it, they saw that it had fully an inch of the extremity of a branch in its mouth, which it had sucked bare of animal matter.

Slowly they drifted along, Long John holding the boat with the grains while they peered into the wondrous garden. Here a huge block

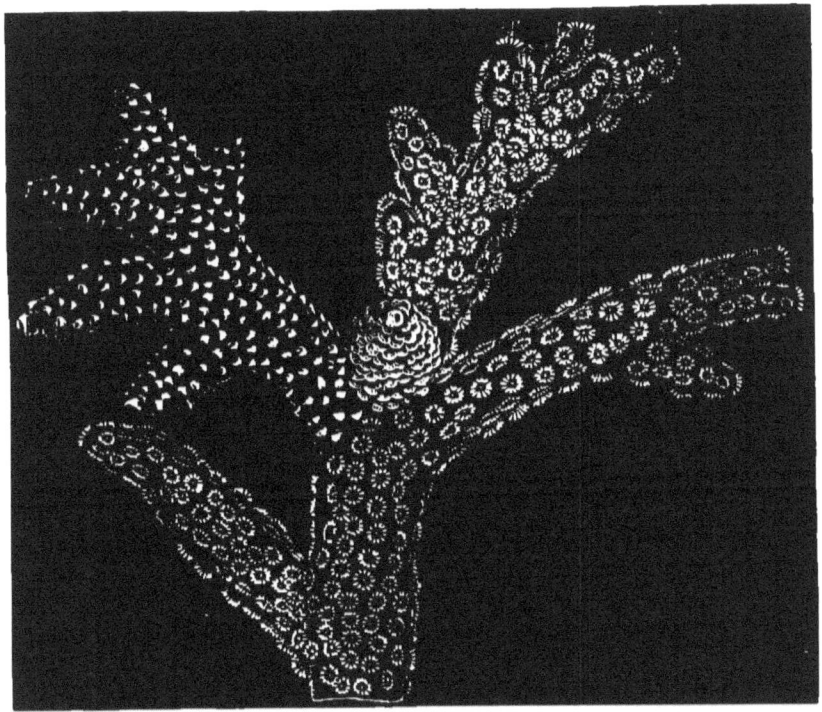

Branch coral (madrepore), showing polyps extended and withdrawn.

of *Astræa,* or star-coral, appeared—a perfect hemisphere, with its polyp flowers all in bloom. The surface in several places showed curious conical plumes, of a pattern like the pompons of a soldier's cap, and colored like them, red and white, in distinct bands.

"These," said the doctor, "are the tentacles and heads of a worm that builds its lime tube on the rock when the latter is small; then, as the coral grows around it, the tube is completely enveloped. As fast as the coral encroaches on the worm it throws out new courses of masonry, keeping pace with the *Astræa*, and vying with it in the exhibition of beautiful tufts of plumes."

Another variety over which they passed had a golden-yellow cup-like series of plumes, contrasting brightly with the brown tints of the *Astræas*.

"The worms are not the simple creatures they are supposed to be," said the doctor. "Look at this evidence of intelligence," reaching over and grasping what appeared to be a bit of weed.

It was the tube of a worm which was standing in the sand. The door was a shell, skillfully inclosed in the masonry, while also fastened to it and falling over was a blade of marine grass (*Zostera*), so that no one would have suspected the true nature of the nest. At the doctor's request the boys went overboard and searched for others. A dozen or more were soon placed on the deck of the *Rosetta*, and every worm was found with the blade of grass inserted as a door—a contrivance employed by some spiders.

"The worms alone would afford us work for weeks," said the doctor, as he picked some fine specimens from the coral and displayed a group of *Serpulæ* on the deck, the tubes being wound together in a singular manner.

The beauty of the corals and gorgonias here caused them to remain for some time, and then they pulled out to an old wreck that lay in shoal water, a quarter of a mile away.

It proved to be the remnant of a very large ship. Part of the lower deck remained, and evidently for years had been a favorite resting-place for the birds. The whole framework was rotten and shaky, and this was found to be due to the fact that the submerged portion of the wreck was literally honeycombed with the tubes of the teredo, or ship-worm. Were it not that these persistent borers had lined the holes they made with a deposit that strengthened the wooden partitions a little, the whole mass of woodwork would long since have fallen to pieces.

After Long John had arranged the contents of the dinner hamper on the dry portion of the deck, and the boys had enjoyed a feast of hard-boiled gull's eggs, craw-fish salad, and turtle balls, which caused them to unanimously confer upon Paublo the title "Prince of Cooks," they continued their search about the old hulk. Suddenly Tom, who was stretched out with his head over the water, where he could observe the fish, cried out: "My, though! there's a queer fish," and the others, crowding around him, saw a large eel-like head bobbing in and out from under a partly imbedded plank. "That's a moray," said Long John, picking up his grains, "and a big one too. Look out there! Let me take a shot at him." Lowering his spear cautiously into the water, he suddenly jammed it into the fish's head, and then, with a quick backward motion, skillfully drew the moray out of its hole. It was over three feet long, and as thick as a man's arm. It made a terrible struggle, twining about the grains, tearing off pieces of the old wreck, and when hauled half-way on deck it fastened its teeth in the wood and held on with the grip of a bull-dog.

"Why, it's a regular sea serpent," said Tom.

"Yes, and there he goes!" cried Long John, as with a loud report the pole snapped in two, and the ugly monster darted away. Tom seized his grains and vaulted to a long head of coral toward which the moray had gone. There he could see the fish writhing about the coral and making desperate efforts to detach the steel barbs. Moving as near as he could, he sent the spear into the moray, and with a vigorous jerk drew it to the coral head, where it leaped and twisted, sending the water in all directions. Long John, in the boat, pushed over to Tom, and soon quieted the struggling fish with a blow from the tiller.

"He's the biggest fellow I ever saw," said he. "Just look at his teeth!"

Their prize was tossed aboard the wreck, and when, soon after, they started for home, the doctor gave the boys some interesting facts concerning it.

"The *Murænidæ*, or morays," he said, "are, as you see, only great sea-eels. They are historic. They were deified by the Egyptians. The Romans kept them in great stews, or storage-ponds, trained them as pets, and held them to be a special delicacy as food. In the time of Augustus Cæsar condemned slaves were thrown to the ferocious fish as food; and when Augustus was declared dictator, one of his courtiers presented the populace with six thousand of these morays taken from his ponds. So you see, Tom, our big captive is worth fighting for and worth preserving."

As the boat was drifting slowly along, Long John suddenly turned to Dick, who was sitting near him, and asked him to take the helm, at the same time cautioning the others not to make any noise, as there was a big turtle near them. The boys looked in the direction indicated, and saw what at first was apparently a piece of lumber floating on the surface, but which turned out to be the back of a turtle. Long John pulled the dinghy alongside, stepped quietly in, and, taking the barbed grains from the pole, fitted on what he called a turtle-peg—a triangular peg about an inch and a half long and looking, as Dick said, like the tip of a file cut off. Fastening the line to the peg, Long John shoved off, and slowly sculled toward the turtle.

The latter was evidently asleep, as it allowed the fisherman to pull within a few feet of it, when Long John dropped the oar, and, taking up the pole, drove the peg into the shell. Up popped the turtle's head; a snort as of escaping steam, and it dived, carrying the line over the side with a whistling sound suggestive of speed and power.

The line was soon exhausted, and away flew the dinghy, Long John slowly pulling in, finally coming alongside, and securing the turtle by its flippers. When the larger boat caught up, the boys lent a hand, and the prize was soon hauled aboard. They were all astonished at this primitive method of taking a turtle; but it was none the less effective, and was the method in use on the reef. The peg simply penetrated the shell half an inch or so, holding by suction, and not injuring the turtle in the least, while if it had been struck with the grains the shell would have been torn and a bad wound the result, rendering it impossible to consign the turtle to the crawl or ship it any distance.

"Did you ever see a sea serpent?" Harry asked Long John, after the excitement over the turtle had subsided.

"Ever see a sea sarpint?" repeated Long John, looking at Harry earnestly with one eye, while the other appeared to wink slyly at the doctor.

"Yes," said Harry. "Have you?"

"I can't say I have," replied Long John, putting on a very wise look; "but Bob Rand has. Bob" he continued, "ain't much of a talker; in fact, I've pardnered with him five years and never held much conversin' with him, but he's a great obsarver—takes in everything, and stores it up like. If he can't tell you about the sea-sarpint, I'm mistaken."

The boys determined to broach the subject to Bob Rand at the very first opportunity.

The boat had now reached the key, and it was fully an hour before the specimens were all cared for. Many were placed in alcohol, others spread out to dry, while tubs and other receptacles held so many that when the boys enumerated them that night, as they sat on the piazza of their cottage, they were amazed at their wealth. In the early part of the evening they cleaned the echini, or sea-eggs, of a former catch;

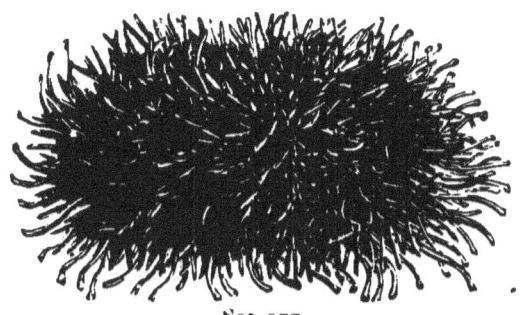

Sea egg.

rubbing and ridding them of their spines with finger brushes, which the doctor had brought for the purpose. After a few days in the sun they presented a white and beautiful appearance, and when placed side by side with specimens having their spines still on, formed a striking contrast.

CHAPTER V.

THE BEATING OF THE JACKS.

The mystery of Bob Rand—The wrecker's opinion—The nest of a fish—Long John expresses an opinion—Bombarded with fish—An adventure with jacks—The mysterious grave—Tom's adventure—Sea-squirts—A school of nurses.

"I FOR one, don't believe Bob Rand knows anything about the sea serpent," said Harry the next morning at breakfast.

"Why?" asked the doctor, smiling.

"Because I asked him down at the wharf," replied Harry, "and he appeared thunderstruck, gave a sort of chuckle, and scratched his head. I almost thought he was going to tell me something, as he stood looking off at the water for at least two minutes, as if trying to remember something; then he appeared to forget all about it, and sculled away, leaving me standing there."

"Bob is a singular character," said the doctor. "Long John, Chief, and Busby, all seem to look up to him as a monument of facts; but I have never heard him say anything. He is certainly very reticent, but is a good fisherman."

"How long have you known Bob Rand?" asked the doctor of the commodore, who just at that moment came in.

"Two years come Michaelmas, sir," was the reply.

"He is a very bright man, is he not?" continued the doctor.

"That he is," said Busby. "I reckon, sir, there's few on the reef that's his ekal."

"On what points?" persisted the doctor.

"Ony pints, sir. I never heard him express himself partic'lar like; but Long John, his pardner, has sounded him, and says there's few like him. It's the general opinion, sir," and the old man hobbled out to get the boat ready.

"Bob Rand seems to have impressed every one with his wealth of mind without doing anything but keep still," said the doctor, laughing; "but, if I am not mistaken, we will find him a faithful comrade as well as an interesting character."

This proved true. Neither of the boys, though living for months with Bob Rand, and out on the reef with him nearly every day, ever heard him enter into any conversation beyond monosyllables, while his usual answer to a question was to scratch his head and look off at the horizon. Yet Bob was an invaluable boatman, the best pilot on the reef, and knew all the secrets of the great shoal.

The tide-gate of the moat, on the southern side of the fort, was a famous place to observe fishes and algæ going out with the current. The morning after their visit to the wreck the boys were seated or stretched along the moat, in various attitudes suggestive of little to do, intercepting numerous specimens floating out to sea.

"Say, boys," said Tom, "wouldn't it be a splendid place to keep a shark, here in the moat?—plenty of water, and no way of his getting out."

"A good plan," answered Dick; "let's do it."

"The place is a good one," said the doctor, "but it means hard work and some risk. However, we will talk with Long John about it. Meantime, when this tide runs out, why not make out to the shoal and find some more sun-shells (*Tellina radiata*) like those Harry discovered yesterday?"

Tellina radiata.

The suggestion was readily accepted, and, while waiting the falling of the tide, Harry, who was lying prone on the bridge, with his face near to the water, said: "These little toad-fish seem to make a nest for themselves, doctor. I've been watching one for some time, and it seems to pick up pieces of dead coral and bits of sand with its fins and tail and then scoop out a hollow and settle down as an old hen does upon her eggs."

Toad-fish.

"Yes, you are right," said the doctor, "it is a nest. Many fishes build such nests. It seems to be a regular hen-like hatching of eggs; and, after the young fish-chicks are out, the parent is as ferocious and untiring a guardian of the children as any hen in a farm-yard."

The tide had now fallen sufficiently to enable the boys to wade out to the shoal, and they were soon at work digging up the beautiful shells. These were marked in a rich imitation of the sun's rays with gaudy colorings. Indeed, Long John firmly maintained that the shells owed their decoration to the rays that shot across the sky during the gorgeous sunsets, for which the locality around the Florida Keys is noted. The sun-shells are in shape much like the soft clams of the North, but wonderfully polished, and ornamented with ray-markings that spring from near the hinge, growing wider as they reach the lip of the shell. They were found at the bottom of a round hole about two inches in diameter and two feet deep, and were invariably dead, with a hole bored in each, showing the death to be the work of some parasitic shell.

"This looks as if the natica, or whelk, had been at work here," said the doctor. "It has a wonderful arrangement of teeth, or grinders, with which it bores circular holes in the clams, and devours them at leisure. By the way, the natica is a nest-builder, such as we were mentioning. Those collar-shaped pieces of sand that you have found on the Northern beaches are the nests in which the natica deposits its eggs."

Here a shout from Long John, who with Bob Rand was out on the sea-wall, caused the boys to look up quickly.

"Look out yonder," shouted Long John; "the jacks are beating!"

Following the direction of his finger, the boys looked toward Long Key and witnessed a singular sight. All around the shore the water was in the greatest commotion, though there was a dead calm elsewhere. Large bodies were seen leaping into the air and falling down into the sea with a noise that could be distinctly heard.

"Why, they're fish!" cried Dick.

"Come on, boys!" shouted Harry; and seizing their grains they all scrambled into the boats and headed for Long Key, which Long John and Bob Rand had now nearly reached.

"Just look at those fish," cried Tom, wild with excitement; "why, there's millions of them!"

He was not far wrong. All along the shore the "jacks"—a species of *Carnax*—had driven in a school of sardines, and so crazed were they with the excitement of pursuit that they were leaping into the air, darting through the solid mass of terrified sardines, and throwing themselves on the beach by hundreds. The sardines literally packed the shore for four or five feet, and out over the water they were leaping in the air, followed by the larger "jacks," who paid not the least attention to the new-comers.

All the party were soon at work in this strangest kind of fishing.

"Give it to them!" cried Tom, as he struck a ten-pounder and flung it on the beach. Dick struck at one in mid-air, and at that moment a large "jack" leaped plump against his legs, so startling him that he stumbled headlong into the mass of floundering fish.

Long John and Bob Rand were standing knee-deep among the sardines, grasping the "jacks" in their hands and flinging them on the beach; but when the boys tried this primitive way of fishing, the sharp dorsal fins pierced their hands and made them bleed.

"You need seasoned hands for this sport," said Long John; and the boys agreed with him.

The "beating" did not abate in the least. Clouds of gulls hovered over the spot and darted down into the mass of fish, while a number of pelicans, including Long John's clumsy pet, were diving among the fish and filling their capacious pouches.

Finally, when all were tired out with capturing this enormous "catch" of fish, and Long John and Bob were at work storing the game in the flat-boats to carry away for cleaning and salting down, the boys climbed into the boats again and pulled leisurely back to the fort.

"This 'beating,'" explained the doctor, on the way home, "is simply the rush of the fish after its prey, and is common to many of the mackerel-like fishes, that become crazed, and, as we have seen, leap entirely out of the water."*

"If you want any shark-fishing, young gentlemen," said Long John, who was seated on a keg, skinning and cleaning "jacks," "now's your time; the heads and backbones I'm chucking over will bait 'em up as thick as mullets."

"I'll tell you what, boys," said Tom, who was stretched out on the sand, "let's put a shark

---

* The "beating" of the Pacific horse-mackerel, or tuna, is a beautiful sight. I have seen a school sweep up the coast, beating acres of surface into foam in their charges after the flying-fish, that, in their fright, flew upon the beaches and even into boats.—AUTHOR.

into the moat this afternoon and see if we can tame him."

"Agreed," replied Dick and Harry in chorus.

"Better look out the shark don't put you inside him!" cautioned Long John.

"Oh, we'll look out for that," answered Tom.

"Well, all the lines are in the boat, and we've plenty of bait here," said the obliging fisherman. "What are your plans for this afternoon, sir?" he asked the doctor, who approached the group.

"I propose we follow up the north end of Long Key, and strike off to the second buoy, where we can try the fishing. When tired of that, we can come in and try the sharks."

Well pleased with this programme, the boys got out the boat, and the party was soon ashore on Long Key. Long John poled the boat along near shore, keeping an eye out for conch or crayfish, which could be used for bait, while the others, preferring to walk, followed along on the beach.

"Hurry up, Dick!" said Tom, giving him a push over into the sand.

"I'll hurry you!" replied Dick, picking himself up and darting after his companion. Although Tom had a good start, Dick was steadily gaining, when Tom suddenly turned, and, running up to the middle of the key, doubled on his pursuer. Harry and the doctor cheered and encouraged the racers, but all at once they saw Tom give a lunge and disappear, and Dick, who was now directly behind, came to a stop just in time to save himself from following suit. As Harry and the doctor reached the spot, Tom was picking himself up at the bottom of a large hollow into which he had fallen.

"Well, that is the worst scare I've had yet!" he said, rubbing his legs. "What is it, anyway?"

"I think I see some bones there," said his father. "Give me your hand, and I will see what it is"; and, steadying himself, he was lowered into the hole.

"This must have been a grave once," he said, a moment later, "for here is a part of a man's skull."

"He must have had a big coffin," remarked Tom.

"No, it is not a coffin, but evidently a very large hogshead, into which the body was thrown. Don't come too near the edge, or you will all fall in."

"I've been here over twenty years," said Long John, who had landed to see what the excitement was, "and never knew any one to be buried here. It must have been one of the old Spanish pirates; they used to lie here years ago."

The boys had heard it whispered that Long John had been a pirate himself once upon a time, and thought he might perhaps explain the strange grave, if so inclined; but he said nothing further.

The doctor took the bones out carefully, but most of them crumbled away. The skull was found to be nearly perfect, but with a fracture at the base, giving the impression that the owner had come to a violent end. The remains were placed together again, and covered with the surrounding sand, probably for the last time.

The sun was now high, and, according to Long John, they were in for a "steamer"; so a start was made up the beach.

"Where can we get some bait?" asked Dick.

"You'll find big-heads and plenty of craw-fish on the edge of the channel, right off the west'ard of the key," replied Long John.

Following the directions, they started; the doctor, Tom, and Harry in the boat, while Dick and Long John waded along the shore—the former chasing spirit-crabs, and picking up shells or bits of sea-weed.

The water on the reef here was about four feet deep, with a bottom of clear white sand, so that any object could be seen upon it some distance away, presenting a scene irresistible to the boys in the boat, who leaned over with faces almost touching the water, while the doctor, with the grain-pole in hand, slowly poled along. Here a big conch (*Strombus*) was lumbering along, racing, perhaps, with the smaller species not a foot away. Now it was a big anemone buried in the sand, and mimicking it in its absence of color; or perhaps a ray was approached, which darted off with a bird-like motion of its fins. It was a perfect panorama, every step offering some new and attractive form.

"What are those round things, shells or stones?" asked Harry, as the boat passed over

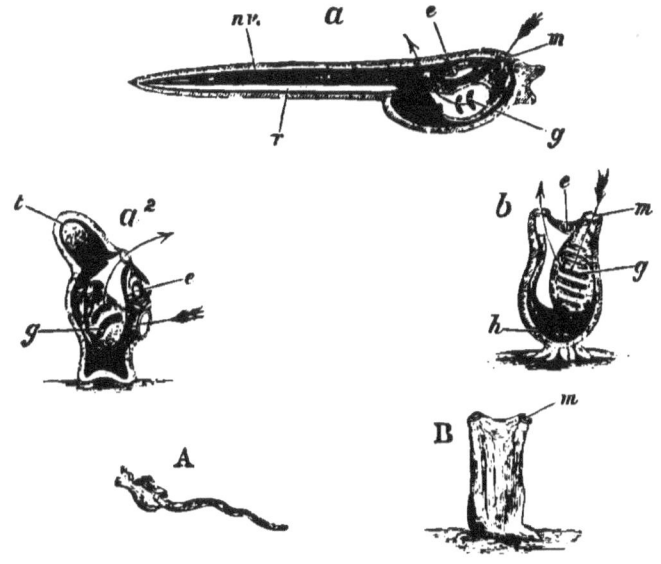

Diagram of the growth of a sea-squirt or ascidian. *A a*, Young free swimming stage. *a²*, Intermediate stage when first settling down. *B b*, Full-grown sea-squirt. *m*, mouth; *e*, hollow brain with eye; *g*, gill slits; *h*, heart; *r*, rod of gristle in free swimming form; *nv*, nerve cord in same; *t*, tail in process of absorption in intermediate form.

some curious oval objects protruding from the sand. "Hold on a minute," he added, and dropped over the side of the boat. Diving down, he inserted his hand under them and brought several to the surface.

"This is an interesting find," said the doctor as Harry clambered into the boat with his prize. "They are called sea-squirts, from their habit of ejecting water. They seem to occupy a position in life between the worm and the lowest back-boned animals. These specimens are what we call ascidians, and they have a most accommodating heart, that, when tired of beating one way, stops, and goes the other, so to speak, throwing the blood in the other direction. Perhaps you can remember them by that."

"Hallo, there are the coral-heads!" cried Tom, who was now poling with his grains in the bow.

"These can't be coral-heads, here," said the doctor, as he looked toward the black spots indicated by Tom; and then he added: "I thought as much. They are black sharks, or nurse, as they are called. Keep quiet, and we can go directly among them. If there is a small one, we might try to catch it."

"Just look here!" cried Tom, growing excited. "There is a regular school, and they're all lying still."

The boat was now directly over the sharks, which were a dark chocolate-color, and many of them apparently over seven feet long. As yet they had not taken the alarm, but, in his eagerness to see them, Tom slipped on the gunwale, and in an instant they all dashed away, stirring up clouds of sand, and rushing by wildly in every direction. Tom could resist no longer, and, as a large one crossed the bow, he let fly the grains.

"Look out!" he cried, paying out the line. "Keep clear of the rope!"

This was more easily said than done, as the rope was rushing out, whirling and turning at a great rate; now taking a turn around an oar and whisking through Tom's fingers, and, finally, in the confusion, twisting itself around Harry's leg and throwing him off his feet. Then the line became taut, and off darted the boat, towed by the shark.

"Take the line off before I'm hauled overboard!" screamed Harry.

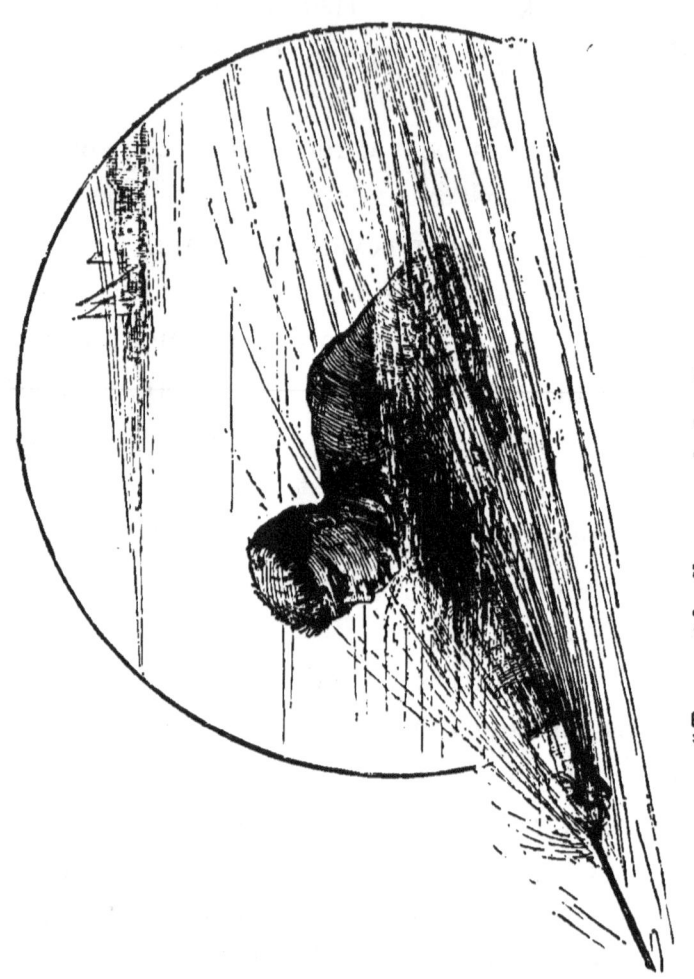

"Tom went headlong over the bow."

The others were laughing loudly over his predicament, but they managed to release him, and again Tom lost his hold upon the line. The rope was nearly run out now,

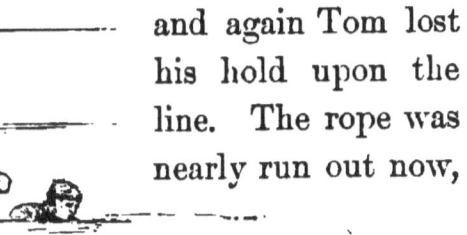

and as the piece of wood to which it was attached dashed over the side Tom seized it, lost his balance, and with the end of the rope in his hand went headlong, with a great splash, over the bow of the boat.

CHAPTER VI.

RIDING A SHARK.

The black nurse—Tom's ride—Graining cray-fish—The coral-heads—The home of the cray-fish—Submarine aquariums—Spearing an octopus—The cloud of ink—Head-footed animals.

FOR an instant Tom was lost to sight, but he soon reappeared, rope in hand, now under water and now above, rushing at railway speed behind his strange steed, which was plowing along, making Tom snort like a grampus.

"Hang on, Tom; don't let go!" shouted the boys. "We'll pick you up."

Tom, who was an excellent swimmer, soon placed himself upon the surface and enjoyed the sport, an occasional cheer testifying that he was all right. The others at once put out the oars, but, though they gave way with a will, they were quickly left far behind. The big fish was headed toward the shoal, and the doctor, seeing that it would probably turn, tried to head it off. Tom occasionally attempted to check his mad charger by striking the bottom with his feet and holding back, but his efforts were useless; he was dragged ahead again, and, when the fish turned suddenly, it became evident that he must either catch hold of the boat or abandon the prize.

"Catch the boat as you go by!" shouted Dick.

On they came. The shark went faster still as it saw the boat, which was now moving in the same direction. A few moments more and Tom was alongside, strong arms hauled him aboard, while the doctor took the line, to which Tom still clung, and made it fast.

All hands now hauled on the line, and the boat was soon directly over the big fish that, after so brave a fight, was beginning to show signs of fatigue. The doctor sent his grains into the shark's head, and with a few sturdy splashes the monster finally gave up the struggle, and was soon towed to the beach and killed.

"That," said Tom, as he leaped ashore, "was the queerest ride I ever had; it even beats riding turtles. What a story to tell the boys at home!"

The shark was found to be eight feet six inches long, and the doctor, cutting open the stomach, showed that it contained sea-weed, holothurians, and the remains of sea-urchins.

"It is too sluggish to catch fish," he explained, "and prefers to root for food, as the pigs do."

Leaving the shark to the crabs, intending to return at another time to secure the curious hinge-shaped jaw, from which it takes its name, the party returned to the boat and pulled away for the cray-fish grounds.

"Here are the coral-heads!" cried Harry, giving the boat a shove to the starboard.

"I should say they were," responded Dick. "Why, they must be four feet across."

"Almost," said the doctor. "You see they look like immense brains deposited on the sand,

and to this appearance the specific name *cerebriformis* refers."

The scene was certainly an extraordinary one. All around them were great heads or domes of coral, three or four feet in height and from four to five feet in diameter. Their color was brown. Some were perfect, and studded

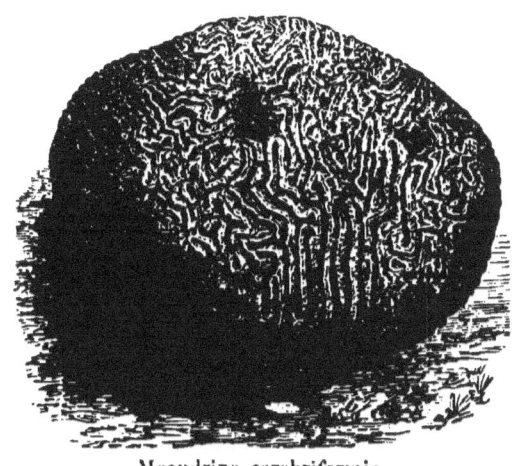
Meandrina cerebriformis.

with the heads of richly colored boring worms, while others were completely worn out in the center, so that they formed enormous vases in which were seen richly tinted gorgonias and fishes of every hue, from the gayly painted angel-fish to a brilliant purple fish that gazed in-

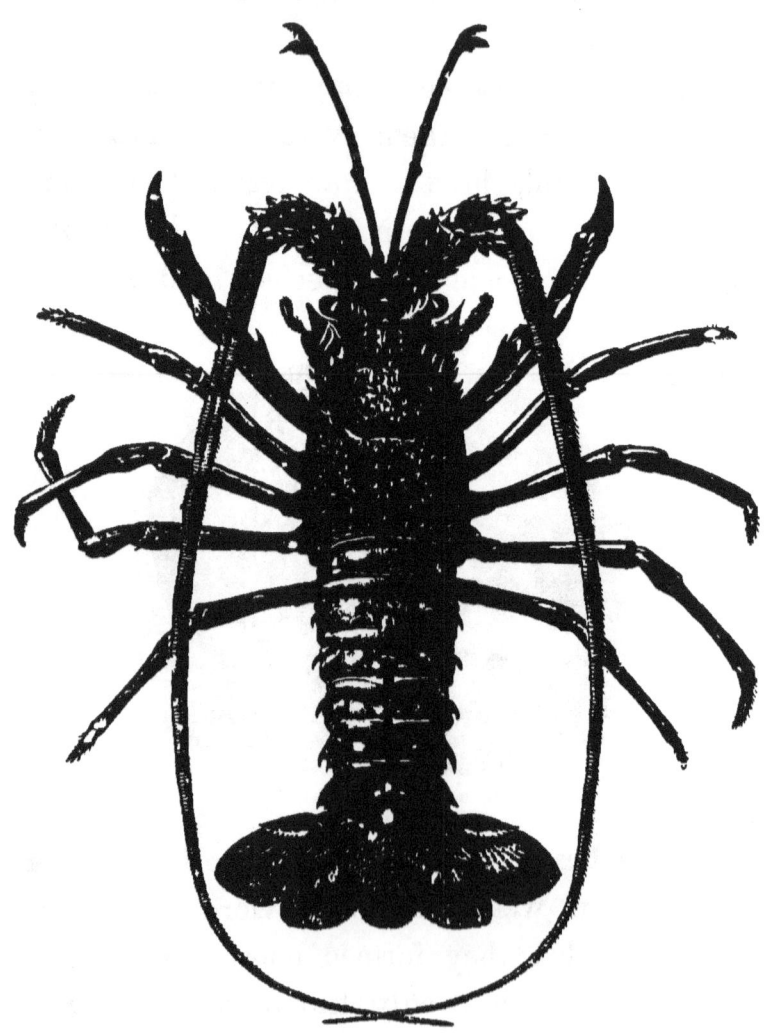

Marine cray-fish.

quisitively at them. The sand beneath the edges of the big coral-heads, as they were called, was dug away by the cray-fish, which backed in, only showing its waving whips or feelers.

"We'll wade along and see if we can find anything new," said Tom, as he and Harry stepped out on one of the heads, taking their grains with them.

So closely were the heads connected that the boys found no difficulty in jumping from one to another, the water being only a foot deep over them, though it was slow work, as they were barefooted, and the peculiar coral borers had raised sharp, jagged points not at all pleasant to step upon. They wandered some distance ahead of the boat, occasionally capturing a cray-fish, and leaving it on the heads for the others to pick up.

Tom had loitered behind to secure a fan-shell that hung from a rich lavender gorgonia, when a shout from Harry caused him to look up. He had evidently struck something heavy, and was pushing and hauling at his grains with all his strength.

"Hurry up!" he cried; "I've caught something or it has caught me, I don't know which."

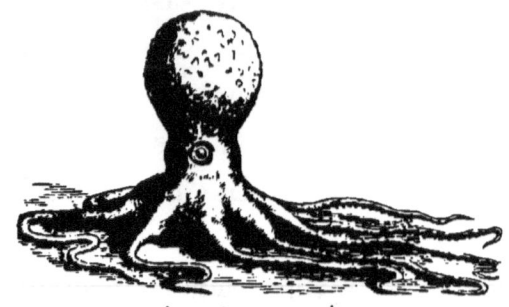

An octopus running.

As Tom jumped on to the head he saw the cause of Harry's excitement. Clinging to the coral was a large mottled octopus; the spear was imbedded in its body, but such was the strength of the animal that he could not move it. The eight sucker-lined arms were fastened upon the rough surface of the coral, while one was wound around the grains. Tom took hold of the pole and jerked as hard as he could, but still the octopus held on like a vise, its expressive eyes almost seeming to flash with rage. Curious waves of color passed rapidly over its body, accompanied by a tremulous motion, while a continuous emission of ink or sepia colored the water for several feet around.

Dick had read some terrible tales of the power of the devil-fish, and as soon as he learned what it was he hailed the boat.

"Look out," he said to Tom, "he'll fasten on to your legs."

"Nonsense!" the latter replied. "Let me get a shot at it."

Dick moved a little to one side, and putting his spear down close to the writhing creature, Tom drove it into him; both then pushed at the same time, and as a result the octopus gave way, winding its arms around both spears. With a jerk they lifted it, squirming and writhing, into the air; and as the *Rosetta* had now reached them they tossed it in.

"That is a fine specimen," said the doctor, holding it down; "but how will you get him off the grains without tearing him all in pieces?"

"Give him a drink of alcohol," suggested Dick, stirring the creature up with a stick.

"A good idea," replied the doctor; "just hold him over this pail."

Long John turned the animal so that its mouth and beak were up, and then a pint of alcohol was poured over it, stupefying the creature so that with a knife the grains were quickly and easily detached.

"Jump in, boys," said the doctor, when the others came up; "we have enough bait, and while we are on the way to the fishing-grounds I will give you a few points on the devil-fishes, as they are called."

"Shake out the sail!" sang out Long John; "and, Mr. Tom, you take the tiller, keep for the middle buoy off Sand Key, and we'll strike it."

The boat payed off before the mild trade-wind, the sail filled, and they were soon under way.

"In the first place," said the doctor, as he settled himself against the sail in a comfortable position, "you must remember that this curious eight-armed fellow, and all the squids, belong to the highest division of the shells or mollusks. They are called cephalopods, from two Greek words meaning 'head-footed.' You see they have a distinct head. Some have their shells within, like the spirula, while others, like the nautilus and argonaut, are protected by a shell.

Argonaut with the shell.

The octopus in these waters seldom attains a larger size than this specimen, or a spread of three feet, though in Alaskan waters they have

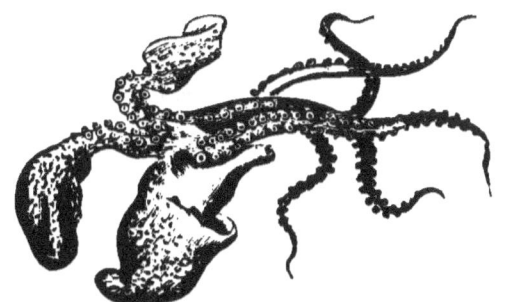

Argonaut without the shell.

been seen measuring twenty-five feet across. The arms, you see, are lined with suckers, and between them are the mouth and bill."

"It's exactly like a parrot's beak," interrupted Tom, who was following his father with his knife on the octopus.

Octopus punctatus.

"Yes," replied the doctor; "the only apparent difference is that the upper bill fits into the lower one, and not over it, as in the birds. The animal lives on the bottom, gliding in and out through the small crevices of the coral with perfect ease, and some varieties have a web-like growth between the arms, with which they swim; but they are essentially bottom animals, throwing out a cloud of ink and escaping under its protection, just as this one attempted to do when you struck it. But here we are," he said, as a big buoy appeared ahead. "I will tell

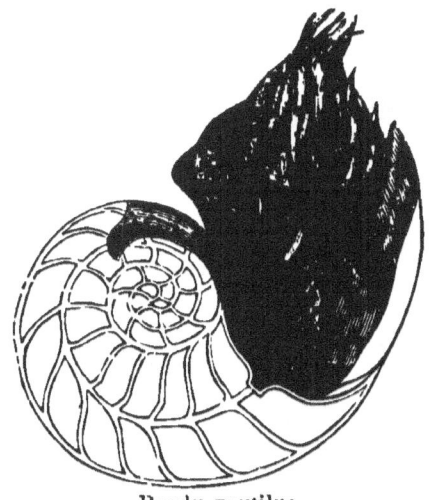

Pearly nautilus.

more about the family some other time, and of an ancestor that was as large as a cart-wheel; and another long, cannon-like one that must have weighed a ton."

CHAPTER VII.

THE TALKING-FISH.

On the fishing-grounds—Exciting sport—Curious catches—The living balloon—The porcupine-fish—Dodging a waterspout—The man-eater—An exciting chase—Tom's adventure with a squid—An ink bath—The talking-fish—Grunts and groupers.

"THIS is the place," said Long John, squinting around to get his bearings.

"Stand by the port anchor!" cried Tom, assuming command with mock gravity and pushing the helm hard down. "Lower away the mainsprit! Let go port anchor! Lay out and furl! Lively there!"

In obedience to these man-o'-war orders the killick was dropped, the sprit unshipped, then the mast, and soon all hands were in various positions and ready.

The lines were mostly smaller than a cod-line, but very strong—the sinker on the bottom, and the hook about four or six inches above it—this rig being necessary in fishing in the coral, the sinker always resting on the bottom, allowing the baited hook to swing clear. Tom had his line over first, and consequently was the first to lose his bait. By the time he had hauled up, the others had all thrown over.

"I've caught him!" cried Dick, giving a tremendous pull. A jerk at the other end sent the line whizzing through his fingers.

"Take a turn around the rowlock," suggested Harry, laughing at his violent exertions.

"No, I have him," repeated Dick; and winding the line around his hand he managed to start the fish. Now he would gain a little, then the fish would get it back; but finally the captive was drawn to the surface, and with a lift brought into the boat. It had an enormous wide-open mouth, and in color was reddish-brown and yellow.

"A grouper," said Long John. "That's a good catch."

Before Dick had taken it from the hook the doctor had landed another, and soon bites were felt on all sides—a success that caused a constantly deepening smile to grow on Long John's red face. The tall fisherman was kept busy preparing bait and killing cray-fish, but he enjoyed the enthusiasm of the boys and shared their delight.

"I've got the bottom!" shouted ungrammatical Harry, drawing up his line.

There was no pulling; the line came in as a dead weight, and in a moment or two Harry had drawn up and lifted into the boat something that looked precisely like a porcupine and was quite as large, at the appearance of which Long John roared with laughter.

"Hey, don't put him near me!" cried Dick, drawing up his legs.

"Is he dead?" asked Tom.

"Why, it's a porcupine-fish—a *Diodon*," said the doctor delightedly; "and a big fellow, too."

The boys danced around in a lively manner to keep out of the prickly fellow's way.

"Good gracious, he's growing larger!" announced Tom. "Give him room!"

The sea-porcupine.

Indeed, the fish was swelling, and in a few minutes was much larger, and as round as a ball.

"He would be a nice customer to meet in swimming," said Tom; and putting the sea-porcupine over, it floated on the water like a rubber ball, having merely filled itself with air.

Harry now landed a beautiful fish with silvery sides and yellow fins, which Long John called a "yellow-tail."

"Hand me that scoop-net, Dick," asked Tom suddenly, fastening his line to a pin. "I've been watching several squids playing around the rudder, and I think I can catch one."

Dick passed the net aft, and Tom, who was sitting on an inverted bucket, leaned over the water and held it in readiness should the squids appear again. They soon returned, and leaning farther over, with his face close to the water, he made a plunge under them with the scoop. But, instead of catching a squid, he started back

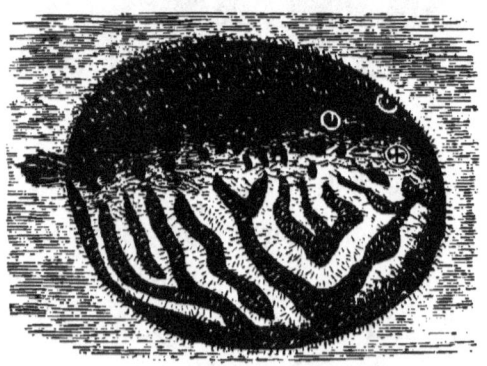

The porcupine as a balloon.

with a loud exclamation, lost his balance, and rolled backward over the bucket in among the fish with a great crash, while the countenance he turned on the rest raised a loud shout of laughter. His whole face was dripping with streams of ink that ran in little rivulets down his cheeks and dropped from his nose.

"What in the world is the matter with you?" gasped Harry as soon as he could stop laughing.

"I suppose the squids shot me," replied Tom, wiping the ink from his face with his handkerchief and trying to smile at the amusement he was affording. "I wouldn't have believed they could throw ink so far," he added. "My face was certainly a foot from the water, and the moment I put the net in I felt the ink. I think I must have dropped the net, too."

"Here it is," said Long John, with a chuckle; "I fished it out. But you did get a dose," he added.

"Well, I don't blame you for laughing," said Tom; "I must look like a zebra. I shall have this handkerchief to remember it by, as they say the ink is indelible."

"I think there is something on your line, Master Tom," interrupted Long John.

Righting his pail and grasping the line, after considerable playing, Tom lifted in a large fish, which no sooner touched the boat than it commenced the most remarkable grunting ever heard from a fish.

"He's a regular talker," said Long John.

"I didn't know that fishes could make a noise," said Tom.

"And, if they do, why isn't it a kind of language?" asked Harry, as he poked the fish, that rolled its red eyes and gave a series of quick grunts.

"It is very possible," replied the doctor, "that they use their voices as do all animals, and in this case it certainly means pain, though some claim that fishes do not suffer out of water; but I do not agree with them. Your catch, Tom, is a remarkable vocalist, but it is by no means the only one. If you have had fishing enough, suppose we up anchor and start for home; we can interview the grunt on the way."

The anchor was soon up, and the *Rosetta* headed for the key. On the way the doctor continued the subject of the "talking-fish," as Tom called it.

"This," he said, "is one of seventy or more known sound-producers among the fishes, and the variety of noises they make would give you ample material for a fish dictionary. They are caused probably by either the lips, the bones of the pharynx, or the air-bladder, and are in many cases involuntary. In the latter class are the fishes known as *Zeus* and *Trigla*, in which the swimming-bladders have a diaphragm which is opened and closed by curious muscles, the operation being accompanied by a murmuring singing sound. The cat-fishes and eels speak, we will say, by forcing air from this bladder into the œsophagus; the former produce a curious crooning noise, while the eels make a somewhat musical sound. It is generally a soft note rapidly uttered, with imperceptible variations, and having a decided metallic ring at times like the distant stroke of a tuning-fork. The mud sun-fish, so common in the Connecticut and Hudson Rivers, makes a sound very similar to the grunt, only in a deeper bass. The gizzard shad utters a loud whirring sound like that of a toy windmill, and the mullet has been heard to utter successive intonations like escaping steam. The hog-fish, found here, and porgy, both make a loud grunting when caught.

"As long ago as the time of Aristotle," continued the doctor, "fishes were known to utter sounds. Sir Emerson Tennent tells us that, while on a visit to the north coast of Ceylon, he heard on the middle of a lake—from whose bottom it was alleged musical sounds issued—very distinctly these same sounds, which were like the gentle trills of a musical chord, or the vibrations of a wine-glass when you rub its rim. The drum-fish make the loudest noises, and on the Jersey coast they call the *Prionotus* pig-fish, because it croaks so loudly when taken in the nets. Prof. Baird believed that these sounds came from the belly of the fish. Travelers have often been startled in their berths by the strange noise of the drum-fish, and I remember that Sir John Richardson says that he could not sleep when off the coast of Carolina on account of the noise these fish made."

"I reckon that's what I've heard often," said Long John, who, while alternately tending the sheet and cleaning up the boat as they sped along, had been an attentive listener. "I remember one night Bob and me was out to the south-'ard here in a calm. We had forgot the oars, and laid there all night, and such groanin' and whistlin' I never heard the like of before. The next mornin' Bob stuck to it that I'd been asleep and had the nightmare; I hadn't, though. But here we are"; and, taking out the boat-hook, the boatman fended off as the *Rosetta* ran lightly alongside the dock.

"War's dat shark dat we was to see swimmin' roun' in de moat?" asked Paublo, who, with some of the colored boys, had come down to help carry up the fish and other specimens.

"We found so many other things that we forgot all about it," said Tom. "When you can catch porcupines on a hook and line," he added, holding up his prize, that had now subsided, "why bother about sharks?"

"I only mention it, Mars Tom, 'case a big

shark's been foolin' 'round here all day waitin' to be cotched," said Paublo.

Further inquiry developed the fact that a dead cow had been thrown overboard, and as it drifted away the men observed several large sharks about it, pulling it beneath the surface, then releasing it, when it would shoot up again, followed by the savage throng. But it was too late to undertake so serious a task, and the sport was deferred until another day.

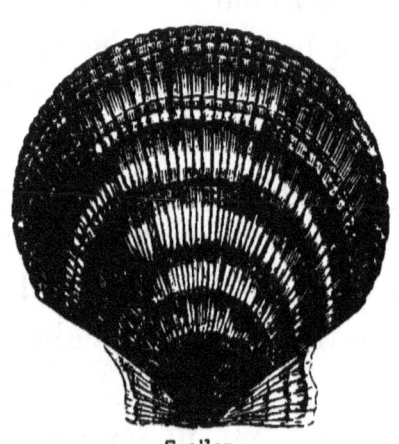

Scallop.

The young naturalists not only delved among the wonders of the shallow reef, but, by using a dredge which the doctor had made, they raked the bottom in deep water beyond the outer reef, obtaining many strange and interesting creatures—delicate crabs and sponges, pectens of an intense vermilion hue, and one crab, also found in shoal water, so blue that it looked like a gem.

Its body was small, with long attenuated legs radiating from it, and its movements reminded

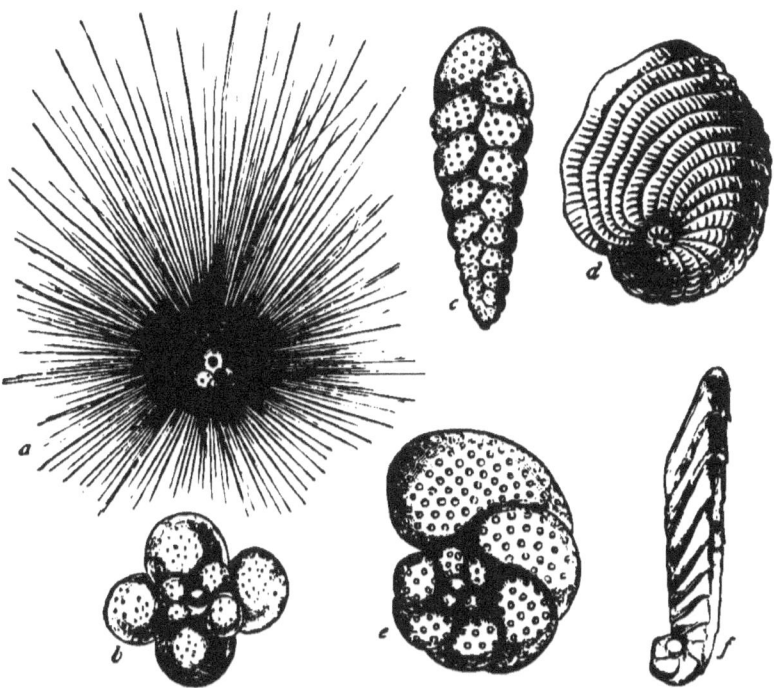

Shells of living foraminifera: *a*, Orbulina universa, in its perfect condition, showing the tubular spines which radiate from the surface of the shell; *b*, Globigerina bulloides, in its ordinary condition, the thin hollow spines which are attached to the shell when perfect having been broken off; *c*, Textularia variabilis; *d*, Peneroplis planatus; *e*, Rotalia concamerata; *f*, Cristellaria subarcuatula. (*a* is after Wyville Thomson; the others are after Williamson. All the figures are greatly enlarged.)

the boys of the toy spiders that work their legs and antennæ. In the mud brought up they discovered many beautiful and curious forms—minute jelly-like creatures (*Foraminifera*) that secrete shells that form a part of the unseen ocean rain. The deep-water star-fishes were especially interesting, nearly all being delicate brittle forms that broke and fell in pieces upon being handled.

The dredge, and especially a drag-net, which was towed astern, brought in many curious fishes floating at the surface; the young of many kinds, which the doctor pointed out, did not resemble their parents in the least; the young of crabs in various stages, known as the *zoëa* and *nauplius*— little creatures with spines and barbs, that were floating in bits of sea-weed. But the most gorgeous creatures were the jelly-fishes, which were often caught in such numbers that they fairly clogged the

Brittle star.

net. They could be studied anywhere, their rich shapes moving here and there over the

Jelly-fish.

lagoon, crystal palaces by day, and at night gleaming with vivid phosphorescent light.

Here was the *Rhizostoma*, a jelly-fish of richly sculptured form, and many more; some like platters, broad and shallow; others bell-like, with long tentacles. Then there were the smaller forms, the minute young in their many shapes; some the offspring of corals, which would in turn deposit eggs that would attach themselves to the bottom, and grow into coral-secreting forms, which in turn would throw off jelly-fishes, illustrating the wonders of alternate generation.

CHAPTER VIII.

THE DISAPPEARING ISLAND.

Tom sees the barracuda caught—Beguiling a fish in the sunlight—Long John's skill with the grains—North Key—The only inhabitant—Wading among the coral—The basket-fish—A suicide—Tom invents a method of classification—Dodging a waterspout.

TOM was up bright and early the next morning, as he had left a number of things undone, and when he reached the boathouse he found Long John just ready to shove off in his dinghy.

"I'm goin' to get a barracuda for breakfast," he said, in answer to Tom's question; "better jump in."

Tom had heard of the big fish, but had not as yet obtained a glimpse of one, so he readily accepted the invitation and seated himself in the bow, while John sculled the boat quietly out into the channel.

The sun was just up—a big gleaming orb that appeared to rise out of the water, dissipating the pink-tinted clouds that lined the western horizon. Long John headed the dinghy directly at the sun, threw over a line about five feet long, to which was attached a white rag, placed his long grain-pole across the boat within reach, then carving off a big piece of tobacco, he solemnly winked at Tom, as much as to say, "Now keep your weather eye open." And this is exactly what Long John meant; so Tom sat still, and watched his tall form working the oar with one hand, and at the same time keeping an eye on the rag that was towing astern.

"You don't mean to say you catch a barracuda with that thing?" said Tom after a few moments, unable to hold his curiosity longer.

"Sartin," replied Long John, with a grin.

Again there was silence, and again Tom's curiosity reached the boiling-point, and he was about to propound another question, when Long John stopped sculling, and reaching down with one long arm seized the grains, then slowly and carefully turned it in the direction of the wake of the boat. Now he gave two or three turns to the oar, shooting the dinghy ahead again; then, with a movement so quick that Tom could hardly believe it possible in any one so long and slow, he hurled the grains at some object ten feet away. The pole came out of the grains-socket, while the line whizzed through the water, cutting it like a knife. A second later a magnificent fish, four feet in length, dashed out of the water, shaking itself violently in a desperate effort to throw off the steel barbs that impaled it. Long John held the line, and it fairly whistled through his fingers as the gamy fish darted this way and that. Now slacking when a vicious rush came, and playing it with marvelous skill, he soon brought it alongside, and with a quick grasp jerked it into the boat, a shout from Tom testifying his appreciation of the skillful capture.

"I'd give a good deal if I could do that," he said, looking with admiring eyes on the beauty.

"Nothing easier when you know how," answered the tall fisherman, breathing hard and coiling his line. "Mighty curious fish," he continued; "I've known 'em to come right alongside of the boat, but generally they keep nine or ten foot off, and when they get in range, why, then I put the grains into 'em. It's easy enough."

"Easy enough for you," replied Tom, "but I don't believe I could do it."

In a short time Long John caught another barracuda, upon which Tom took the oars and pulled the dinghy in. Dick and Harry were both down at the wharf waiting for them.

"See what you miss by lying in bed!" shouted Tom, as they drew near, holding up a big fish.

The barracuda were slung on an oar, and, placing the ends on their shoulders, Tom and Harry started up the walk to the cottage, and soon the odor of broiling barracuda arose from Paublo's department.

"The barracuda must be one of the quickest of all fishes in its movements," said Tom, after describing the rushes of the big fish as he had seen them.

"You are right," said his father; "but how fast they can travel would be difficult to determine. The speed of a salmon has been estimated at forty feet a second. The barracuda is more perfectly fitted for speed than the salmon; its long pointed head, powerful fins, and rakish dorsal fin remind one of a yacht built for speed."

Though the barracuda was so easily caught by the skillful handling of the grains, it is, in reality, one of the most wily fish, as well as gamy, to be found on the reef, and an inexperienced hand might fish all day without success. The smaller ones, from a foot to eighteen inches long, are excellent eating, and were found in great numbers in the shoal waters of the key, or hanging on the outskirts of schools of mullets and sardines into which they would occasionally dash. Tom finally became very skillful in catching them. He used a very fine line rigged for the purpose, the hook attached by a long piece of the finest copper wire without a sinker. If live bait was not at hand, Tom was capable of making a dead sardine struggle as if alive. When he saw a barracuda he would hurl the line beyond it to one side, the bait being gradually dragged in its direction. Soon the attention of the game was attracted, and at it he would dart, but not to bite. The cunning barracuda merely dug its nose into the sand and backed off, eying the bait with a critical gaze. Now all depended upon Tom. If he could induce the barracuda to believe the bait was alive and trying to escape, the fish was his; but, if the work was clumsily done, the barracuda would turn tail and swim away in disgust. A delicate twitching at the line invariably produced the desired result; the barracuda darted again at the bait, and after nosing it several times finally took it deliberately and moved away; three or four convulsive swallows and the bait disappeared, whereupon the hook was jerked into it, and the latter end of the sport commenced.

"I don't believe Long John was ever a pirate if he can catch a fish the way Tom said he did,"

Dick remarked, as they stood on the shore after breakfast, waiting for the doctor.

"Nor I either," said Harry; "he must have been a fisherman all his life."

As they spoke, the doctor appeared, loaded with a box of phials for specimens, and the boys hastened to relieve him.

"I am going over to North Key," he said, "the most northwestern key of this group, and interesting because it is a key just forming or disappearing—it is difficult to tell which. After a severe hurricane, the men tell me, a sloop could sail over it, but during pleasant weather it appears out of water again."

The boys were always ready for an excursion, and going aboard Long John's fishing-boat, which he called the *Bull-pup*, because she clung to the wind so, were soon bowling along, headed in the direction of the island. After an hour's sail they sighted it—a patch of white sand, bearing a few grasses, and so low that it was evidently swept during heavy gales. The *Bull-pup* was anchored near shore, the boys and the doctor taking the dinghy and pulling in, hauling it upon the beach, after which they explored the limited area.

"North Key," said the doctor, as they stood on the sands and looked about, "may be considered the last of the chain of islands to the north in the waters of the Florida Reef. You see there is no mangrove growth here, owing, perhaps, to the strong winds which prevent the seeds from taking root; and, besides, the winter northers sweep the ridge raised by the summer trades, and level it so that for several months in the year it is often entirely under water."

The boys were impressed by the singular sight of an island dependent upon wind and wave, and Tom christened it Disappearing Island, as it was always coming and going. A few clumps of grass grew here and there, the growth of seeds washed ashore. Even the spirit-crabs, generally the first to take up a residence, were absent. The white shore showed a few stranded sea-snails, while delicately outlined were the tracks of a sea bird, whose footprint here was almost as astonishing as the one found by Robinson Crusoe. The key was deserted. No, on the very summit of the low ridge a solitary gull's egg was discovered.

"Not much, certainly, to furnish instruction or entertainment," said the doctor, "but it shows that even here a purpose has been served, and one of God's creatures has found a home."

There was no attempt made to rob that home, and the egg was left to be hatched by the hot sun and bring forth the little gull that would certainly be the Robinson Crusoe of the birds, as Tom said, and in full possession.

The reef off shore offering more inducements, the party boarded the boat again, and after a sail to the south came to anchor on the edge of the channel.

"How low the water is!" said Dick, pointing to the tips of branch coral which appeared above water. "Suppose we wade out, boys."

"Very well," said the doctor. "Take the dinghy to put your finds in, and John will attend to the lunch, after which we can try the fishing."

Shoving off the dinghy, they waded along,

dragging the boat, there being just water enough to float her without them. The coral was nearly all a madrepore, with short branches growing in clumps, forming quite distinct but winding channels all over the reef; in these the boys kept, the water not being over knee-deep. Their method of taking specimens was to tear up a bunch of coral and lift it into the boat, upon which the crabs, star-fishes, shells, and sea-eggs, that made their home there, would drop off, and those that clung to it could be picked off, after which the coral was exchanged for another bunch.

"Good gracious! what's this?" exclaimed Harry, who had lifted up a bunch of coral on which appeared something that looked like a ball of snakes slowly twisting and coiling in every possible position. As he raised it the curious arms commenced to drop apart, falling into the water in a perfect shower.

The doctor, who was watching Harry, laughed heartily at the ludicrous appearance presented by the discoverer. Afraid to drop it around his feet, or to move, there he stood, holding at arm's length the writhing mass that was rapidly decreasing in size.

"Get it over the dinghy, quick," the doctor said, "or there won't be anything left. It is only a star-fish."

Harry secured what remained—merely a round body, with several arms. "I thought I had a nest of young sea-serpents," he said.

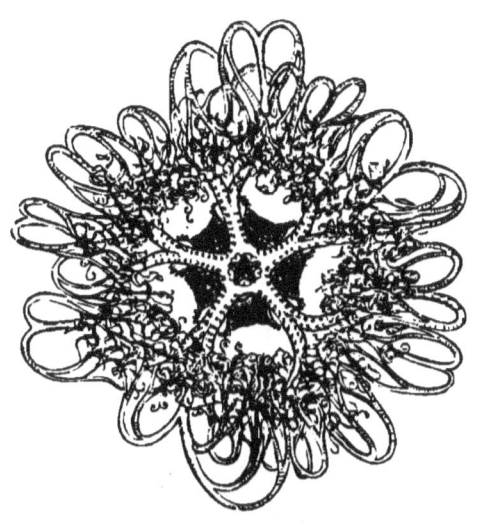

The basket-fish (*Asterophyton*).

"It is the basket star-fish," explained the doctor; "and these are its arms, branched in every direction, and certainly snake-like."

"But what made it break up?" asked Harry.

"It committed suicide; a number of animals do the same. The only way to save them is to drop them instantly into alcohol after they leave the water; otherwise they throw off their arms and tentacles, as you have seen. As it is, we have not much left of this one."

"If I had my way," said Tom, who had been trying to pronounce *Asterophyton*, the name of the star-fish, as they rested upon the coral heads, "I wouldn't have any long scientific names for any animals, but just call this a basket-fish."

"That might do very well for you, Tom," replied his father, "but the scientific names, as you call them, are very necessary. Suppose now you had discovered a new star-fish, and in your description called it the basket-fish; when the French, German, Italian, and other scientists read your report they would have no little difficulty in finding out what you meant; so for this reason scientists decided many years ago to adopt a common language. Latin was the one selected, though Greek words are also used.

This simplifies matters, you see, as this language is known everywhere."

"I see," said Tom, "and I don't believe my system of classification would do."

"What is it?" asked his father, laughing.

"Why, I should put all the long-nosed fishes together, as an example."

Sword-fish and saw-fish.

"You would have a strange mixture," replied the doctor.

"Why," continued Tom, "there is the sword-fish, saw-fish, bill and trumpet fish, snipe-fish, spoon-bill sturgeon, and narwhal."

"But the narwhal is not a fish," rejoined the doctor. "See what a confused arrangement you would have. Now, what are called pouched animals you would think would be all alike;

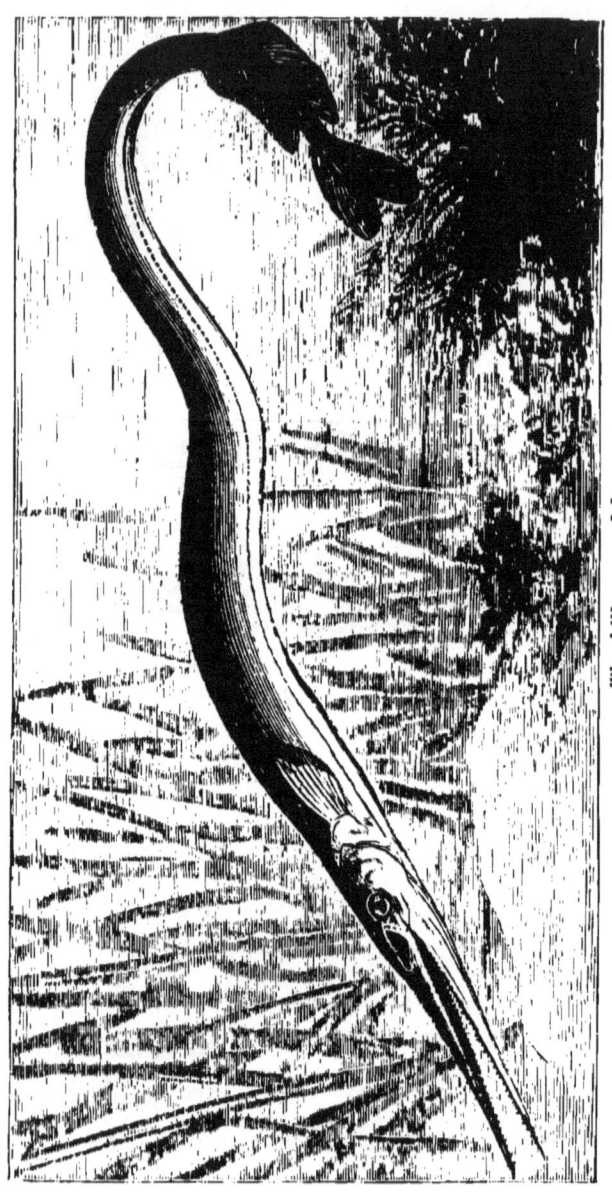

The bill or gar-fish.

but they show the greatest variation, though a great many entirely different animals have pouches. For instance, there are the kangaroo, opossum, some of the tree-toads, the pipe-fish and sea-horses, an echinus, some of the cat-fishes, and many others totally at variance as regards structure. So you see your plan would hardly work."

"If you young gentlemen don't object," interrupted Long John, who had been an attentive listener, "I think you had better come aboard"; and as Tom and Dick waded toward the boat he pointed behind them. A long, low, lead-colored cloud had appeared so quickly that they had not noticed it, and from it two curious points extended down.

"Jump in quick!" cried the doctor; and the boys wasted no time, but floundered to the boat, and, following Long John's directions, got out the oars and put them over the sides of the clumsy sail-boat.

"What is it?" asked Dick.

"Them's waterspouts forming," replied Long John; "and as they have killed the wind, and might bother us, I want to be ready. We could pull the sloop away from them if they came this way."

The boys had seen the full-fledged waterspout, and now had an opportunity to see the

The sea-horse.

formation of these ocean monsters. Down came the points until half way to the water, when they noticed another column rising from the surface up to it. It was a wonderful spectacle, and they sat resting upon their oars almost spellbound. In a very few moments the two portions joined, and the perfect waterspouts began to move away.

Now a gentle wind sprang up, and the giants bending toward the direction of the wind, Long John took the helm, and slowly the *Bull-pup* filled away, passing not two hundred yards from one of them. They saw how easily a ship could be destroyed by contact with one, and would be almost powerless to escape.

The waterspouts moved grandly away, and, taking advantage of the fresh breeze that appeared to come from the cloud, they bore away for home, Dick and Harry holding trolling-lines in what proved vain hopes of taking a king-fish.

CHAPTER IX.

TOM AND THE MAN-OF-WAR.

A pirate's island—The parrot-fish—The queen conch—Mimics—The file-fish—Floating nests—Tom takes a lesson with the cast-net—Catching a flamingo—The race—Tom succumbs to the Portuguese man-of-war—Long John blows up the man-of-war—Wonders of phosphorescence.

A FEW mornings after this excursion the expedition, under Long John's guidance, was making a run across to East Key, some eight miles from the fort. The sky was richly tinted with crimson from the rising sun, that seemed reflected everywhere. Shoals of fishes sprang from the water. Dark-hued rays darted aside in graceful curves, the musical cry of the laughing-gull sounded above, and every living thing seemed enjoying the beautiful morning.

They rapidly crossed the channel, by Sand and Middle Keys, and in an hour were on the great reef that surrounded East Key. The wind had died away entirely, and a dead calm left the sails hanging straight and lifeless.

"Well," said the doctor, "I'm afraid we shall have to pull for it. But it is only about three miles to the key, and, by working slowly along, we may pick up some specimens."

Long John, who was sculling the dinghy alongside, kept pace with the larger boat, and his watchful eye saw many a choice specimen that their inexperienced eyes would have overlooked. The water was about fifteen feet deep, and so clear that the smallest shells could easily be seen from above as the boats drifted leisurely along.

"See those angel-fishes; how they resemble birds!" said the doctor, pointing to a number of them gliding in and out among the coral branches. "They sweep down, a score at a time, as if they were a flock of birds-of-paradise; and there is a parrot-fish. Steady a moment!"

"It seems too bad to kill this beautiful creature!" said Harry.

"But one may be spared for a specimen," said the doctor, preparing the fatal alcohol. Then he showed the boys how wonderfully the saws of the *Scarus* are adapted for grinding coral. The teeth, they noticed, were incorporated with the bone, and grew crowded together in groups of five.

"No wonder they are named after the parrot," said Dick; "they are like them in color and in beak."

"There goes a beautiful fish!" exclaimed Tom, pointing to a yellow one with blue stripes and a black spot on its tail.

"It is one of the *Chætodons*," said the doctor; "they are so evenly balanced that it is difficult to distinguish the head from the tail. They are commonly called 'four-eyes.'"

"It's a good name for them," retorted Tom, having hurled his grains ineffectually. "They are too keen-sighted to be caught."

Here a shout from Long John, who had sculled ahead, drew their attention, and pulling up to him they found that he had seen a rare shell—a "queen-conch," or *Cassis*. It lay at the bottom of a shelving bank among some large shrub-corals. The great mollusk seemed almost elephantine as it glided along the smooth surface, its large proboscis, like the trunk of an elephant, extending far before it. Its mound-like shell seemed covered with a checkered cloth; and, indeed, this is the soberest part of the *Cassis*, the gorgeous colorings being upon the under surface or shield-like face which drags over the mud.

Tom, who stood on the bows of the boat, swaying to and fro, suddenly tumbled over into the gulf. As the ripples cleared, the boys could see him far below, peering cautiously among the coral branches. Dick plunged in after him, and soon both boys had deposited the great conch in triumph in the boat. It proved a grand specimen for the aquarium. The great conches, when in the cabinet or on the mantel, are handsome objects, but they are perfect marvels of beautiful coloring when first taken from the water.

"You'll find plenty of crabs and things in this," said Long John, hauling a little field of floating gulf-weed alongside.

Dick secured it, and they captured several specimens of the *Antennarius*—the nest-builders first seen at Marquesas.

"Why, here's a crab," exclaimed Dick, "right under my eyes! And here's another lying on the weed, and a fish with a file for a fin."

"It is not strange they escaped your notice," said the doctor. "They are mimics, and see how exactly in color they resemble the weed. This is a provision of Nature for their protection. These animals are what is called pelagic in their nature, floating around in the Gulf Stream carried by the weed. Now, if colored like some other crabs, the first gull that came along would swoop down and carry them off; but Nature looks out for this, and has given them tints in exact imitation of a patch of the surrounding weed, and you will notice that even the little zoöphytes that grow upon the weed are imitated. So with the fish," continued the doctor, taking one up. "See the yellow, green, mottled colors, its curious barbels and fringed fins, how almost exactly they resemble the *Sargassum*. If you did not know what you were looking for, it would escape notice, so complete is the deception. A large number of animals are afforded protection of this kind, while others use their natural advantages to obtain food. Some time to-day I will try to give you a further account of some of them."

"Hold hard a second!" cried Long John suddenly; and reaching under the seat he hauled out a cast-net. With a quick motion he threw it over his left arm, wound a cord about his wrist, and, taking another portion of the net in his mouth, motioned the boys to pole toward a school of fish. Wondering how anything could be caught from such a confusion of meshes and sinkers, they obeyed. When within reach, Long John swayed his body to the right, and swinging the net to the rear, with a sweep he hurled it from him. It spread out in a circular form about ten feet in diameter, and came down with a crash among the mullets, covering at least two thirds of the school. The skillful developments of its powers elicited a shout of admiration from the party. Long John gave several jerks at the line he still held that secured the struggling fish, and as they came up he lifted the catch aboard, when the construction of the net was seen.

Though in use on the reef, the cast-net is probably of French origin. When spread out, it is circular, the circumference being lined with oval sinkers. At the axis of the net, supposing it a circle, was an opening through which passed eight cords that radiated to different parts of the circumference. After passing through the aperture at the axis, they joined and became a single cord, of any length, that is held in the hand when the net is thrown. When held up, the net hangs like a closed umbrella without a handle, and, when cast, falls like an open parachute. No little skill and practice are required to make it fall perfectly open; this having been done, it will be seen that a few twitches at the cord will tend to haul the different parts of the circumference, which has now become the bottom, up toward the axis, now the top, until the fish are entirely encompassed and can be lifted from the water completely enveloped in its folds.

The operation looked so simple that Tom was anxious to try it, and after some directions from Long John he took the net over his arm, grasping several of the meshes in his teeth, and, with one foot on the gunwale, with more force than skill he hurled the net. The catch was heavy. The flap that swung behind him caught over his elbow, and the sudden pull upon his teeth forced him ahead, and amid the roars of the party over he went in a confused tangle into the water, from which they extricated him as soon as they could.

"Caught yourself that time," said Long John, with a chuckle, as Tom came up, feeling of his teeth.

"Yes," he answered, "and came near being my own dentist. I think I'll practice on shore before I try it again."

Later, the boys, under Long John's instruction, became expert cast-net throwers, and it was invariably used in taking the mullet and various bait-fish.

Drifting along, the boat soon reached East Key—the coral bed, over which they had been passing, coming to a sudden end a hundred yards from the beach, and giving place to a clear, pearly, sandy bottom.

"Give way with a will!" said the doctor, clapping his hands. The oars bent in the water and, with a rush, the boat was sent high on shore, where all speedily hauled her above high-water mark. Long John took out the sails to rig up a tent, while the boys followed with the hamper and the frying-pan. As they came ashore, innumerable bright-colored crabs were seen to run up the beach and suddenly disappear.

"Spirit-crabs!" cried Harry; but it seemed an inappropriate name for these singular, square-bodied creatures, which were of the same color as the surrounding sand, into which they burrow quickly, sallying out by hundreds, when danger is past, to feed on whatever is washed ashore.

Tom had heard a story of some pirate's gold being buried on East Key long ago, and his curiosity was roused.

"I believe I'll take a look for that gold," he said.

"We must all go, then," said his father, laughing, and starting ahead. As the nearest way to the east shore was through the brush, they found an opening, and struck into it in Indian file at a slower pace. The bushes were low and thickly tangled, and it proved hard work to push through. Hermit-crabs hung on the branches, and the sand was so undermined by land-crabs that the walking was uncertain.

"Here's an opening," cried Dick, and with much satisfaction they were just about to pass through, when, with a great rustling, seven or eight large flamingoes rose in air just before them. Tom, with ever-ready gun, blazed away at them, and brought one down; it fell like a rocket-stick on Dick's head. The great bird was uninjured, except that its wing was broken, and Dick found it no mean antagonist, receiving several hard blows from its blunt bill before he could grasp the snake-like neck. Finally, however, he secured the bird by the neck and legs, and the party moved on to the beach.

"Don't flamingoes build nests like mounds?" inquired Harry.

"Yes," replied the doctor, "they make a nest like a column, and sit on it as do other birds. The nests are high or low, as the case may be, but that they sit astride the nest, as some claim, is a fable."

As they came upon the beach the doctor, shaking the mangrove leaves from his coat, said,

Flamingo and nest.

with a laugh: "Now, Tom, here is a half-mile of sand to turn over. If you expect to find the pirate's gold before night, you had better begin."

Tom thought the prospects scarcely promising. "I believe I'd rather take a swim," he said. This suited the rest also. Long John, who had just rowed around in his dinghy, hauled it up on the beach, and he and the doctor threw themselves on the sand, while the boys went into the water. The beach shoaled off here, as on the other side, with a hard coral bottom, coming to the living coral about a hundred feet off shore. The boys had become expert divers from continued practice, and now arranged themselves in a row, four or five feet distant from one another, in order to see which of the party could swim farthest under water.

"Are you ready?" asked the doctor.

"All ready, sir," they replied.

"Well, then—go!" he called; and at the word "go" the row of boys disappeared beneath the blue waters in a simultaneous dive. Less than half a minute brought two of the swimmers to the surface for breath. A few seconds after, Tom's head appeared quite near the coral belt. His victory was hailed with cheers, but, instead of striking out for shore, he gave a terrible scream, for an instant seemed trying to tear something from his body, and then sank out of sight.

As Tom disappeared beneath the waves, Dick and Harry, speedily recovering from their first surprise and fright, struck out for the scene of danger. But Long John and the doctor were already in the dinghy, and with a few powerful strokes passed the swimmers and reached the spot soon after Tom appeared at the surface.

"A man-o'-war stung him!" exclaimed Long John.

"Keep back, boys!" cried the doctor, waving the swimmers away, and together he and Long John lifted the apparently fainting boy into the boat.

Poor Tom presented a terrible appearance. Upon his arms and the upper part of his body a blue, jelly-like mass of tentacles had fastened themselves and seemed eating into the flesh. Long John seized the boat-sponge and rubbed off the slimy mass, while the doctor forced a restorative down Tom's throat. The greater part of the blue slime was soon washed off, and then Long John, taking his knife, scraped the skin as hard as he dared. A bottle of oil was poured over the poisoned parts and brought much relief to Tom, who began to show signs of recovery.

An hour later, as he lay on the shore under the shade of the mangroves, weak but comparatively comfortable, he said, in reply to a question from Long John:

"I came up right under it; I felt as if I had fallen into the fire, and then I must have almost fainted away."

Portuguese man-of-war.

"You're all right now, though," said Long John; "I was caught in the same way myself once."

"Here's what did it," said Dick, holding up a stick upon which hung something that looked like a bubble attached to a long mass of blue streamers.

"What is it?" Tom asked.

"It is the *Physalia*, or Portuguese man-o'-war," said the doctor; "one of the most beautiful of all marine animals, and at the same time, as you can testify, one of the most dangerous. It is a mere bubble that floats on the water, dragging these tentacles after it. They are covered with minute cells, and when touched throw out millions of barbed darts, carrying with them the blue poison which, as you see, covered you with a network of lines."*

"Why do they call them 'men-o'-war,' doctor?" inquired Henry.

"Because this membrane on the top can be spread out by the animal, and, when the wind catches it, the *Physalia* bowls along like a man-o'-war under full sail," the doctor explained.

"Some men-o'-war blow up," said Long John;

---

* This was the author's experience, and I carried the marks for nearly a year.

"and so does this!" and, giving the *Physalia* a blow, he exploded Tom's uncomfortable assailant, which burst with a loud report.

"Those tentacles into which Tom ran," continued the doctor, "can be lengthened or drawn up at will. They are the fishing-lines of the animal. When a fish touches them he is killed as by an electric shock, and then hauled in among the tentacles nearer the body and absorbed."

They sat for a long time in the shadow of the mangroves, discussing the *Physalia* and other curious and kindred forms, until Long John told them that the night camp was ready. By this time, Tom being able to walk without help, the party left for the camp, where an excellent supper of turtle meat, gull's eggs, and fried grouper awaited them. After watching the gorgeous tropical sunset, the mainsails and foresails were unshipped with the masts and hung over the bushes for a shelter, as they had concluded to pass the night on the key. Before this impromptu tent had been arranged it was eight o'clock. It was a fine night, and a slight breeze rolled gentle waves upon the sands with a musical intonation.

The party were stretched on the beach, which was still warm with the sun's rays, when the curious appearance of the water attracted their attention. Wherever a wave broke or threw off its pearls of spray the water, as if by magic, assumed a ghostly, cream-like tint; and, as the night grew darker, the entire sea glowed with a moving, golden light. Waves of fire broke upon the beach, drops of liquid flame hung upon the bits of coral or dropped from them like streams of molten lava.

"There is an uncommon sight," said the doctor, rising and walking toward the water. Soon the whole party was wading in what seemed to be a gleaming sea of fire that fairly blazed at every step; and, as they walked along, splashing the water right and left, the effect was indescribable. The doctor now proposed that they row out to study this phenomenon. The rowboat was shoved off, and, jumping aboard, they pulled out through a blaze of fire that with every dip of the oars seemed, as Dick said, "to light up the sea all around." Taking a tall specimen-glass, the doctor filled it from the sea of fire and placed it on a thwart where all could see it.

"Now you can see what makes the light," he said, pointing out numbers of round animalculæ. "They are *Noctilucæ*—the same that we saw at Marquesas. See how the light changes. Sometimes we catch a blue or yellow gleam, and then it deepens to a rich green."

The boat slowly drifted to shoal water again, and now the scene below them was still more animated. Here a large jelly-fish was moving about in a basin formed of leaf and branch corals, throwing a beautiful light among the branches, lighting up the homes of the zoöphytes and making the fishes cast dark shadows. Scores of delicate *Medusæ* moved up and down, or in and out, with as many different motions, each gleaming with a subdued, steady light.

"They are like satellites revolving around a larger planet, are they not?" said the doctor. "They may well be called the light-houses of the sea, as one of you suggested."

182 ALONG THE FLORIDA REEF.

"Why, I declare, boys," exclaimed the doctor, some time after, looking at his watch, "it is after eleven o'clock. We must return to camp—such as it is."

The oars were manned and the rowers bent to them, passing silently through a golden river of their own making.

After reaching the shore the light-givers were laid aside for alcohol baths on the morrow, and soon after the tired party sought their primitive beds.

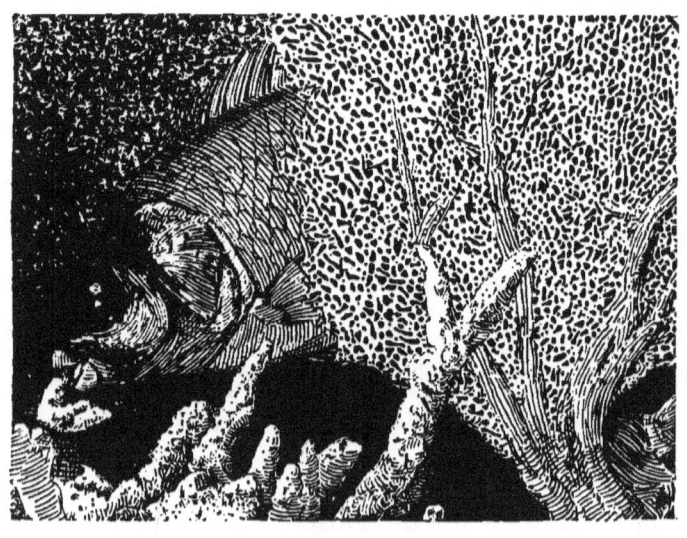

Parrot-fish (*Scarus*).

CHAPTER X.

THE MYSTERY OF EAST KEY.

Tom has a remarkable adventure—The mysterious stranger—The surprise—Following up the trail—General Tom leads the army—Pirates and doubloons—Jack Tier—The sea-horse—Small conchs—Collecting shells.

TOM'S adventure with the Portuguese man-o'-war did not tend to render sleeping on mangrove and bay-cedar leaves an easy matter, consequently he was up long before sunrise, and to pass the time before breakfast he wandered down the beach, listening to the musical ripple of the waves as they broke upon the sands like so many bell notes.

He had walked possibly a quarter of a mile along the beach, when, seeing an opening in the bush, he strolled in, led by the sweet odor of the bay-cedar and possibly to see how far the path led. He had not gone far when he saw an object that almost made him shout with astonishment. In the dim light was the figure of a man on his knees, digging with both hands in the sand. Tom knew that the island was uninhabited, or at least that it was supposed to be, and the thoughts that rushed through his mind of pirates and Spanish galleons would have made a chapter in this recital. Alarmed and surprised at the apparition, he stood for a moment rooted to the spot; then, fearing that he would be discovered, he backed cautiously into the bush, still keeping his eyes on the figure that was evidently engaged in excavating something. Tom decided to drop to the ground and creep away under cover of the bay-cedar, and so regain the beach, when he could quickly make his way to camp and inform the others. He was about to put this resolution into operation when the figure rose up and quietly disappeared in the bay-cedar forest. After waiting a moment, that seemed an hour, Tom quickly retraced his steps and in a short time rushed breathlessly into camp.

The boys and the doctor were still asleep, but Long John was preparing to build the fire, when he was startled by the appearance of the excited young naturalist.

"Didn't you say that no one lived on this island?" he asked breathlessly.

"Sartin I did," responded Long John, dropping his armful of wood and turning his red face on Tom with an expression of amazement.

"Well, it isn't so," retorted the latter; and then he rapidly related his experience to the fisherman and the others, who, awakened by the talking, now gathered about him.

"It's sing'lar," said Long John, taking off his hat and rubbing his head, as if feeling for an idea.

"Very," echoed the doctor, who had been studying the luminous face of their guide and boatman. "Are you not mistaken, Tom?"

"Certainly not, sir," replied Tom. "I saw the man not thirty feet from me, digging in the sand, and as plainly as I ever saw anything."

"Who could it have been?" asked Dick.

"I propose we find out," said Tom, bravely picking up his gun.

"We'd better all go," said Long John. "It's five to one, and I reckon we kin take him."

He then picked up his grains, which was perhaps a habit, the others took their shot-guns, and the little army moved off up the beach, led by General Tom, presenting a decidedly warlike appearance.

It did not take them long to reach the opening in the bush, and as they drew near the spot Tom pointed triumphantly to the impressions of feet in the sand, and then a cavity a foot or more deep.

"Something has been here, surely," remarked the doctor.

"Looks that way, sartin," replied Long John, examining the sand carefully. "You're sure it wasn't a turtle?" turning to Tom.

"A turtle wouldn't stand up and walk off, would it?" asked the latter.

"No, it wouldn't, that's true," admitted Long John.

"Here are a man's tracks leading into the bush!" cried Dick.

"Let's follow them up," said Tom, excitedly, and into the bush they pushed, Indian file.

There had evidently been a path here at some time made by egg collectors, but the bush, nearly ten feet in height, had grown together, so that it was necessary to push it aside; but as the tracks were distinct they went ahead rapidly.

"What do you suppose is the matter with Long John?" whispered Tom to Harry after they had gone a hundred yards. "Do you see how he lags behind? He can't be afraid, can he?"

It apparently looked as if Long John did consider discretion the better part of valor, as nothing but the top of his grain-pole could be seen.

"What should we do if the man should attack us?" asked Tom of his father.

"Better try arbitration first," answered the latter.

The path wound in and out, and as the

tracks grew more distinct the bush grew higher.

"I don't know which way we are going," said Tom, "but I think I hear water."

"Yes, and I see it," said Harry. "The trail leads out to the beach here. Whoever it is probably has a boat, and we shall come out where it is hauled up. Here we are," he added, coming to a halt; "let's all push out at once." After waiting a moment for Long John, the party moved quickly forward and came suddenly out upon the beach.

"Why, it's our camp," exclaimed Tom, evidently dumfounded; "we've come back to it."

He stood still a moment; then, hearing a snort, turned his eyes upon the tall figure of Long John, who was standing with his back to him, supporting himself upon his bending grain-staff and evidently laboring under some strong emotion.

Tom walked quietly up to him, and, after one glance at his face, redder than ever, he burst into laughter, in which all joined at his expense.

"Then it was you," he said, throwing down his gun.

"I believe it was," answered Long John, rubbing his head vigorously, "and I reckon I've had a narrow escape."

"But what were you doing up there?" continued Tom.

"I wasn't digging gold at four o'clock in the morning," replied Long John, laughing, "but I was gettin' water. You see there aint no water on the key, so I keep a demijohn filled and buried up there in case I ever git caught here in a norther, and I was digging for that demijohn when you came upon me. There it is," he added, pointing to the innocent cause of all the excitement.

"Well, I suppose I'll never hear the last of this," said Tom good-naturedly, and Dick and Harry assured him that he never would.

"The way I came to put the water here," said Long John in further explanation, "I was off the key fishing with Bob once, and a squall came up and sent us ashore; then it turned into a norther and blew for three days before we could get off, there was such a sea running. For the last two days we had no water to speak of, and I made up my mind I would never git caught again; so I keep the demijohn hid here, and as we had plenty of water in the boat, I went up to fill it this morning."

"Well, if we haven't found the pirate's gold, we have had some excitement over it," said the doctor.

"There used to be pirates enough here in old times," said Long John. "I never found any gold myself, but there's a story going around the reef that a big Spanish treasure ship went ashore on the east side of the key one hundred years ago, and that the old light-house-keeper picked up twenty thousand dollars in doubloons; but I never see any of it, so can't say for sartin."

"These islands must have been a famous rendezvous for the old Spanish freebooters," said the doctor. "Cooper, the novelist, evidently thought so, as here he laid the scene of one of his novels—Jack Tier."

After breakfast a trip was made up the west beach, where they found a fine collecting-place for shells, and filled their pockets with many beautiful kinds. They wandered over the sandflat that extended all around the island, and dived overboard from the boat, bringing up various treasures. Dick discovered a large horse conch, probably the largest shell on the reef, while in one place they found a colony of a small species of *Strombus*, about the size of one's closed palm; the back of this was rough, while the interior was beautifully tinted. The big *Strombus gigas* was seen everywhere, the shells ranging from the big broad-lipped fellows to younger ones in which the lip had not begun to turn. This was the shell that jewelry is made from, and that is supposed to furnish pink pearls, though our young naturalists failed to find them.

Among the discoveries were another attractive conch—a *Fusus*—and a rough *Triton*. In some places varieties of *Pecten* and a *Trochus* were very common, while a minute pink shell was especially abundant.

While looking over some weed Harry found the first sea-horse—*Hippocampus*—a singular little fish with a horse-like head and a prehensile tail that clung to the weeds. The little creature made no attempt to escape beyond moving his fins, and was transferred to a glass, and finally to the aquarium, where he was kept some time.

The doctor gave an interesting account of the habits of this little creature, and pointed out the marsupium or sac in which the males carry the eggs until hatched. He told them of a sea-horse, a wonderful mimic, with long streamers like sea-weed, that had been caught in Australian waters.

Near where Harry found the sea-horse Dick noticed a curious object, of a greenish tint, that looked like a bird divested of its feathers. It was soft, and when touched emitted a rich purple ink and moved two wing-like folds. Long John said it was a sea-pigeon, while the doctor, who had joined them, pronounced it one of the shell-less mollusks—an *Aphysia*. "In ancient times," he said, "these animals were called sea-rabbits"; and certainly there was a resemblance, as the *Aphysia* had now regained its upright position and was moving about its glass prison on the deck of the boat, showing a head and long ear-like appendages. This patch of weed also produced the long spiral egg-case of the horse-conch.

After a small but valuable lot of specimens had been collected the boat bore away for home, the party well satisfied with their trip to the largest key of the group.

CHAPTER XI.

THE ISLE OF BIRDS.

The black cloud—What it was—Collecting eggs in barrels—Eggs in the air—The noddy—Some wonderful mimics—Flying fish—A narrow escape from sharks—Wonderful sea-weed—A discovery—The pirate's cannon—Diving after a relic—The movement of shells—The silk of shells—Robber crabs—Decorative crabs—Tom leaves the party.

"HOW would you like some eggs for breakfast?" asked Long John one morning at daybreak, as the boys were turning out.

"No turtle-eggs for me, if you please," laughed Harry.

"I don't mean turtle-eggs," rejoined Long John.

"Has the pelican been laying?" asked Dick, as he came out.

"Come here, and I'll show you the kind I mean," answered Long John, who was standing at the south window. Following the direction of his long finger, they saw a dim cloud hanging over Bird Key.

"What is it?" they asked in chorus.

"What is it?" repeated the fisherman; "why, that cloud means birds, and eggs just as good as hens' eggs."

Taking the glass, Tom saw what were apparently thousands of birds wheeling over the island. "That *is* a sight!" he exclaimed, handing the glass to Dick. "Why, there must be a million!"

"Where do they come from?" inquired Harry, who was always ready to ask questions.

"From all over," replied Long John. "They've been here two days; but I thought I wouldn't say anything and give 'em a chance to lay; to-day you can git all you want."

The young naturalists had been so long on fish and turtle diet that they were delighted at the thought of a change, and after breakfast they rushed down to the boat, where they were joined a little later by the doctor and Long John.

"What are you going to do with that, Mr.

Tom?" asked Long John, smiling, as Tom tossed a small basket into the boat.

"Put eggs in it," was the answer.

"This 'ere's the kind o' basket you want," said Long John, lifting an empty flour-barrel into his dinghy.

"Do you expect to get that *full?*" asked Tom.

"Well, I reckon," replied the fisherman, shoving off the pelican, that expressed a desire to go with them. Tom said nothing, but looked exceedingly doubtful.

As there was no wind, they took the oars, and slowly pulled along the channel toward Bird Key. Dick stood in the bow, grains in hand, on the lookout for anything new. A long shoal extended out here toward Bird Key, forming the southwest channel. Along its edge they skirted, passing groves of branching coral, heads of *Astræa*, and again the broad leaf-coral. The reef fairly teemed with life, and oars were often dropped and the boat allowed to drift slowly along, her occupants, with faces near the surface, watching the panorama below.

The water gradually became deeper, but, owing to its clearness, they were enabled to distinguish small objects at a depth of nearly fifty feet.

They had almost neared the stake buoy, where they crossed the channel, and were about to resume the oars, when Harry cried "Stop! back water! see what that is on the bottom."

Peering over, the others saw lying in the short grass, and hardly distinguishable except to a keen eye, a long, dark object.

"Can you make it out?" asked Tom, straining his head over so far that the boat tipped.

"It looks like a log, or a piece of boom or mast," said Dick.

"*I'm* going to find out what it is." So saying, Tom began pulling off his outer clothing. "Stand by with your grains and don't let the sharks eat me," he said.

"There are no sharks here," retorted Long John.

"Hold on, then," said Dick, "and I'll go with you."

The boys were soon ready, and while the

boat was steadied they dived down. When the water had cleared, the lookers-on saw them swim rapidly to the dark object. Then they evidently touched it, as a cloud of mud or sand almost obscured them from view. Hardly half a minute elapsed before they both appeared and were at the surface, hanging to the boat, puffing and blowing.

"It's an old cannon," said Tom breathlessly; "I've discovered something piratical this time surely."

"Where do you suppose it came from?" asked Harry of the doctor.

"It may have been from one of the old pirates," he replied.

"It is covered with weed and coral," continued Tom; "but if that was scraped off we might find a mark on it. Here goes!" and he again sank beneath the surface, followed quickly by his companion.

This time they dug the sand away from the gun, and when again at the boat the hole they had made by its side exposed the cannon to full view.

"There will be no trouble in getting it up," said Tom, climbing into the boat; "only take the bearings of the spot, and we can come back for it."*

"The two chimneys on the quarters are just in line," said Long John. "If you remember that, you can easily find it again."

"Your conch is bound to be a cabin passenger, Dick," said the doctor, as a huge mollusk, which the former had brought up from the side of the gun, gave a lurch and hauled its shell along toward the stern with a half-leap.

"It must be hard work traveling that way," Dick remarked, pushing the conch over upon its back to see its sword-like operculum.

"Still, they make very good progress on sandy bottom," replied the doctor. "The mollusks are queer travelers. The *Donax* moves along by sudden leaps, just as this conch does. The river mussel, which you remember has the curious marsupium for its young, progresses by a climbing movement of its so-called foot,

---

* The gun was placed in Fort Jefferson, and is probably there now.—AUTHOR.

but the common scallop dances through the water by rapidly opening and closing its shell;

Common salt-water mussel.

and when a party of them start off they look exactly as if they were dancing through the water. Many other shells float along the surface, and depend upon the currents and winds for their movements. The stilifer snail, like one of Tom's pirates, boards the star-fish and sea-urchins and is carried by them, while many others are peculiar to the gulf-weed, and either go the grand rounds with it or become a fixture in the great Sargasso Sea. But the great-

The dancing scallops.

er number of bivalves are forced to lie in one spot, trusting to the currents to throw food in their way. Such are the oysters, and on some grow spines that hold them so that the waves will not wash them about. Some build grottoes and lattices, thus imprisoning themselves. Other shells burrow deeply in the mud, and others again weave cords of silk to which they fasten themselves."

"Is it really silk?" asked Harry.

"Sufficiently like it to be made into articles of ordinary wear. If you ever visit the British Museum, you will see gloves and other articles made from the silk of the pinna. The threads are fine and of great strength, and when mixed with about one third real silk spun on the distaff, form a material of a beautiful brownish-yellow color."

A noise, heard slightly at first, but now increasing to a roaring sound, interrupted the doctor, and as they neared the key it was evident that it proceeded from the black cloud, which began to show its true nature to the astonished party. In a few moments the noise was so great that they could hardly hear each other speak. As they drew near, the birds flew at them with wild cries, as if determined to stop them, then turning suddenly to fly back and rejoin their companions.

As the boat ran on to the white sandy beach the uproar was indescribable. The gulls dis-

Oysters, showing different stages of growth.

puted every inch, flying down and darting into their very faces. Tom uttered a loud cry and the effect was remarkable. In an instant it was perfectly quiet, not a sound being heard, the great mass of birds sweeping down in silent fear, as if to listen. But it was only for a moment; then the confusion recommenced and seemed greater than before.

After Long John had rolled out the barrel they started into the brush. The island was about a mile around, and, like East Key, completely covered with bay-cedars, forming a close brush nearly ten feet high, interspersed here and there with patches of prickly pear. Under it on the sand the speckled eggs lay in such quantities that hardly a step could be taken without breaking them.

"I think we had better sweep them up," said Tom; but he had hardly spoken when down came an egg, dropped by a bird frightened from her nest, striking him fairly on the head.

"You'd better get a net if you are going to take them that way," shouted Dick.

"I didn't think it would rain eggs," retorted Tom laughingly, and wiping his hat.

The boys went down on their hands and knees and piled the eggs together, while Long

John filled the barrel, carefully placing leaves between each layer.

The eggs were laid in a slight depression in the sand, made by the gull, that left them to be hatched by the sun. Besides the immense numbers on the ground, almost pure white eggs were found on the top branches of the bushes, laid by the noddy—a lovely bird, with dove-like eyes expressive of gentleness, a dark body, and white head. The nests were on the very top of the slender bushes, and in but few instances did they appear to be hollow, the single egg being held in place by the twigs.

"See here, boys," shouted the doctor, putting his hands to his mouth that his voice might reach them.

The egg-collectors stopped, and, approaching, found him standing in a little pathway that led into the bush. The doctor pointed to a large, stout spider's web that spanned the path, and asked them if they saw the spider. They all shook their heads, as it was almost useless to try and talk in such an uproar.

"It is right before you," he shouted. They

looked again, and then witnessed a remarkable performance. A big, gorgeously-colored spider appeared in view, clinging to the middle of the web. Upon touching the network, the spider, a clever fellow indeed, raised its big body and imparted to the web a swinging motion that rapidly increased until the acrobat almost disappeared from view, on the same principle that the eye can not follow an object moved to and fro with extreme rapidity.

Ocypoda, a marine-crab that lives on land.

Dick raised a cheer at the spider's cunning, and some time was spent practicing on what Tom termed the magic spider, until, convinced that it was found out, it dropped to the ground and moved away. There were numbers of these spiders here, and the doctor called attention to them as illustrating a most interesting method of protection. If an enemy, as an insectivorous bird, approached, the spider could almost immediately render itself invisible.

As the doctor had encouraged the boys to discover protective resemblances, this was an interesting addition to a number of mimics they had found.

Later Tom found a cactus or prickly-pear branch bearing the ripe fruit, and clinging to it one of the big purple land-crabs (*Gecarcinus*) common on the keys. He was trying to obtain the fruit, and did not notice the crab clinging to the leaves until he almost touched it, which the doctor pronounced a most interesting instance of protective resemblance. "You can see, boys," said the doctor, "the application of this: the crab was certainly protected by its resemblance to the fruit for the time being."

Dick had the cast of a shell of a white spirit-crab on a patch of white sand to illustrate its habit and another example, and the doctor pointed out the fact that these crabs were never seen away from the white sand or in the bush where it was covered by the yellowish leaves of the bay-cedar, while the purple crab was never seen away from the interior or upon the domain of the spirit-crabs. It was Harry's good fortune to discover the most remarkable mimic. The day previous, observing a very large *Physalia* or Portuguese man-o'-war floating near shore, he had gone out in the dinghy, at the doctor's request, to measure its tentacles. He found them drag-

Gecarcinus rusticola, a land-crab.

ging ten feet, being lowered down into a school of sardines, and as he was watching he saw the method of fishing adopted by this dangerous creature. Above the surface a beautiful bubble with all the luster of satin and the tints and hues of the rainbow—a gem of the sea; but from the lower portion depended a bunch of intense purple tentacles which could be lowered down to a greater or less distance. Harry distinctly saw a sardine dash from the school and bite at the tempting bait. The instant of contact, over it turned as dead as if struck by an electric shock; in fact, as the doctor afterward showed them, its delicate scales were perforated by thousands of minute barbs that were shot out from lasso-cells in the tentacles of the man-o'-war, and the shock had killed the victim, that was then hauled rapidly up to be eaten by this singular creature.

To better examine it and see how far the sardine had been drawn up, Harry lifted the *Physalia* out of the water by its satin-like sail, which could be done in safety, and then made his discovery. The moment he lifted the bubble he saw four or five little fishes dashing wildly about. They had been beneath the death-dealing *Physalia* and now were evidently much alarmed. He placed the *Physalia* in the water again, and immediately the little fishes swam back to it. Placing his face near the surface, he saw distinctly the fish hovering up under the bubble surrounded by the tentacles, and extremely difficult to distinguish from them, as they were of almost the exact tint of the tentacles—a rich purple—and in this resemblance found protection.

This led to the examination of other Portuguese men-o'-war, and one was rarely found without the little attendants.

This instance of mimicry was a remarkable one, and Tom added to it by finding little fishes beneath large jelly-fishes, all having pink and white tints, affording them protection by the resemblance.

The boys were infatuated with this feature of natural history, and almost every day added to what they called their collection of mimics. The little attendants of the jelly-fish and *Physalia* were all members of the mackerel family, famous for seeking protection beneath other animals.

Having heaped up all the eggs they could carry, the boys wandered down to the beach again, where Long John had just hauled ashore a cast-netful of fine mullets.

The day was warm, and after lunch they crept under the bushes and rested an hour, watching the wonderful sight of unlimited thousands of gulls in the air.

"Look here, boys," said Harry, who had been watching a bay-cedar; "here is a grand example of a struggle for existence!"

He was standing by a noddy's nest, upon which was a young bird—a queer featherless

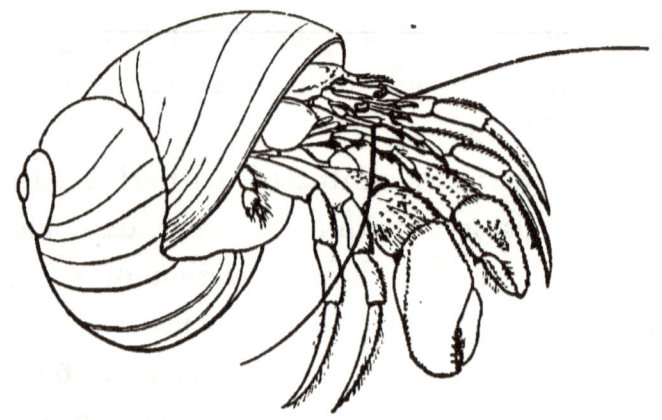

Marine hermit-crab.

little creature; and overhead the mother was wheeling around in evident despair. She had liberally provided her young with a large sardine—too large, in fact, for it to eat; and hanging on the nest, in all conceivable positions, were a dozen or more land-hermits and two large purple-backed land-crabs. One of the latter had the tail of the fish in its claw, while the hermits were tugging at the head; others were crawling around the defenseless bird as if trying to make up their minds whether to attack it or not.

"I should think it *was* a struggle," said Tom, giving the nest a shake. "Why, they're regular robbers!"

"Worse than that," retorted Dick; "as they steal from children, I think the noddies must be kept busy if they have to feed their young and all these crabs."

Tom and Dick now started up the beach to see an old wreck, while Harry and the doctor followed along through the bush. The latter had gone but a few yards when they found several flying fishes caught in the bushes and dried in the sun.

"They couldn't have flown here, could they?" asked Harry.

"No, they were probably dropped by the gulls when chased by the large man-o'-war hawks that you saw hanging so still in the air over the light-house the other day," replied the doctor. "The gulls catch them, and the hawks trying to steal them, they probably fall here."

After a short walk they reached a point where the boat was in sight, and found the rest

Frigate-bird.

of the party waiting for them. All being ready, Long John shoved off, and the doctor proposing that they make a tour of the island, which was agreed to. As the water was very shallow, the boys preferred to wade along and pull the boat —a plan that suited Long John, who lighted his pipe and began to clean the rest of the mullets for supper.

They had gone but a short distance when Harry held up a spider-crab, which he had taken out of the coral, and exclaimed: "This is an old stager! He has a regular forest on his back."

The crab was, indeed, well covered; sprigs of purple and red sea-weed growing from its back, while its claws were bedecked with a soft sponge, several barnacles, not to speak of tube-making worms that had taken possession of other portions.

"He is one of the decorators," explained the doctor; "pass him over, and I will show you how they ornament themselves."

Harry passed the crab to him, and taking a finger-brush, which they used to clean shells, he began a vigorous rubbing on its back, evidently much to the creature's astonishment, and soon had it clean and free from the various growths.

"Now, give me some little pieces of sea-weed," he said, dipping the sea-spider into a glass of water. These were soon forthcoming, and dropped in the glass with the crab.

"Now," continued the doctor, "these crabs are instinctively aware that the rays and nurses, and many other fishes, have a weakness for them as articles of food, so the question naturally arises in the crab's mind, 'How can I protect myself?' Its movements are slow, so it can not run; its claws are inadequate as a defense, and you would think the old fellow in a desperate strait. But somehow it occurs to him that moss-covered rocks are not molested by the fishes, so he evidently says: 'I will become one of these rocks to all appearances.' Nature has helped him, you see, with a rugged exterior, and—but I need only refer you to the crab himself for a justification of my remarks."

While he had been talking, the old crab had felt all around its prison and now was proceeding to carry out the transformation the doctor had predicted. The long claws, with great deliberation, picked up a sprig of the weed they had thrown in, and slowly passed the root or severed part to its mouth.

"He's eating it," exclaimed Tom.

"Wait a moment," said his father.

The branch was pressed against its mouth, and then, instead of eating it, the crab raised it over its back and pressed the severed end against its shell, then removed its claw, leaving the weed attached to its back as if growing there;

The decorator.

then another piece was taken and the operation repeated many times. The boys felt very much like cheering the crab for its wit and cunning, and before they reached home it had an assortment of algæ upon its shell.

This proved an experiment the boys were delighted with, and it was remarkable how well concealed the crabs became by the operation that is by no means confined to the crabs of the Southern seas. Now wading, pushing the boat through the narrow passages lined with coral, and anon jumping aboard and rowing over the deeper places, stopping to dive down after some choice shell or coral, the party gradually completed the circuit of Bird Key, or the Isle of Birds, as Tom named it, and shoved off into the blue channel that led toward home.

As they neared the fort, Tom, who was at the helm, steered the *Rosetta* near a spile that took the place of the buoy, and as they passed by he stepped upon it and the boat shot on.

CHAPTER XII.

CATCHING A MAN-EATER.

Tom's narrow escape—Preparations for the sport—The struggle and capture—Falling on a man-eater—In the moat—The prisoner and provost-marshal—The hermit-crabs—A wonderful assemblage—The animals on the island.

TOM'S idea was to perpetrate a joke upon his companions. They were all facing the bow of the *Rosetta*, and he assumed that they would not miss him for some seconds or until the boat came up in the wind, and then would be astonished at his absence.

Such was the case. The *Rosetta* glided on for some distance, then, naturally, came slowly up into the wind, and as the luff of the sail quivered and then flapped, the occupants looked around and were dumfounded for a moment in finding that Tom was gone; then, seeing him standing as straight as an arrow on the pile, they raised a shout.

"You'll have to swim for it," called Dick, taking the tiller. "Turn about is fair play."

Tom was somewhat disconcerted at the turn his joke had taken, as the fort was a quarter of a mile away and deep water nearly half the distance. He called for them to come back, but they laughingly held on their course, leaving him monarch of all he surveyed. Finally, seeing that they intended to make him swim for it, he began to take off his clothes—a difficult operation while standing on a platform about eight by ten inches. He had divested himself of his shirt and trousers, and was about to fasten them upon his head preparatory to lowering himself into the water, when a shout from the *Rosetta* caused him to stop. Looking up, he saw that the boat had gone about and was now coming back.

"Hold on!" shouted Harry, who was standing in the bow; "look at that!"

The blue shark.

Tom looked in the direction indicated, and saw, not one hundred feet away, between him and the fort, several large fins slowly cutting the water.

"See what you were going to swim into," said the doctor, as they came up, pointing to the sharks that, re-enforced by several others, were now playing around on the top of the water.

"Well, I'm glad I didn't start," replied Tom as he jumped aboard, "though," he added, "I don't believe they would have touched me."

"*I* wouldn't risk 'em," said Long John; "this might be just the time."

"Suppose we get the eggs ashore and catch one for the moat this afternoon," suggested Dick; "we've talked about it so long."

"Good!" responded Tom. "But can we haul him in?" he asked Long John.

"Yes," the latter replied. "I looked at it this morning, and it's high tide this afternoon, so you can easily run one over—that is, if he don't haul you over first," he added.

"Well, we'll try it. Give way, boys!" cried Tom, and the boat shot ahead and was quickly run alongside the lower dock nearest the quarters.

After the eggs had been disposed of on shore the shark-lines with several groupers were thrown into the boat with a coral-hook as anchor, and the boys started off again, poling along in the direction they had observed the sharks.

Upon reaching the spot the boat was laid alongside the branch-coral that fringed the channel, and the long coral-hook thrust into it instead of an anchor, as it could be easily pulled up and cast off.

Tom baited one of the lines with a headless grouper, and, swinging it around his head several times, launched it out into the blue water where the sharks had been seen but a short time before.

"Now throw over these old heads and gills," said Harry.

Tom did so, and then, after seeing that the line was run through a hole in the cut-water, sat down to wait.

They were chatting about their many experiences when a splashing was heard astern, and some of the bait that had drifted there was seen to have disappeared; then a faint jerk came on the line.

"He's taken it!" whispered Tom hoarsely, as if afraid of frightening the fish.

"That was a crab!" said Dick.

"No," Tom insisted; "they bite that way, gently at first. Here goes the line anyhow."

Sure enough, the rope commenced to run slowly out.

"Stand by the coral-hook!" cried Tom to Dick, slackening out. "Long John said to give him about fifteen feet, and when I jerk, cast off and see that the line isn't foul. Keep your knife ready to cut, Harry, if we get into trouble."

Dick and Harry took a good hold on the line; then, when the fish hauled it taut, all hands jerked the hook into it with all their force and so much energy that Harry, who was last on the line, went backward down among the bailers, oars, and bait.

The astonished shark hesitated a moment, then darted off like a shot, tearing the line from their grasp and giving them a lively dance to keep clear of it.

"Look out for your legs and keep amidship!" screamed Tom, taking a turn with the slack. "Steady, steady! look out!"

His warning came not a moment too soon; the line was all out, and as it came taut suddenly the boat lunged ahead with such a terrific jerk that they all went down except Tom, who was well braced in the bow.

"It must be a big fellow," gasped Harry, picking himself up the second time.

The boat was rushing up the channel at a rapid rate, the bow deep in the water, and a small tidal wave running ahead, not at all pleasant to contemplate.

"It's a big one, sure enough," said Tom, who, red in the face from trying to keep the line in place, stood, knife in hand, hesitating whether to cut the line.

"Get in the stern, all hands, or he'll pull the bow under," said Dick.

"Cut the rope!" cried Harry, as the boat gave a suggestive lunge, water coming in.

"The line's broken," answered Tom, as the strain let up suddenly and the boat righted.

"That's a shame," he added. "No it isn't. Look out for yourselves!"

As he spoke, the line came taut again at right angles to the boat. The shark had only changed his direction, and the jerk pulled the boat down so that the water poured in by the bucketful.

"Get to windward quick!" shouted Tom; and they all rushed to the other side just in time to escape a capsize.

The boat now darted ahead as before, burying her bows in foam, and moving around the channel toward the fort.

"We're going the right way now, and must try and take in some slack," said Tom. "Take hold! That's it, now!"

Altogether they grasped the line and hauled away, starting the shark to more furious exertions. But they kept at it; now gaining a little, then losing, till after ten minutes they had the fish, a perfect monster, in sight.

"Here comes the doctor," cried Harry in a relieved tone.

He was in a dinghy with Long John and Bob Rand, rapidly nearing them.

Tom got a line ready, and as they tore by he hurled it at the dinghy, and soon their fiery steed had two boats in tow instead of one.

"I was afraid he was too much for you," called the doctor, hauling in on the line; "but he can not stand this long."

Tom was taking in every inch, and in a short time their boat was directly over the shark's tail. "Now a long pull!" he cried.

The boys surged on the line with a hearty "heave o'!" and ran over the shark. Another brisk turn, and they had its head partly out of water and on its side. But the shark had not given up yet; the great scythe-like tail beat the water with terrible strokes, and twisted in every possible position in the attempts to break away, showing a mouth full of white serrated teeth which it ground together in a most unpleasant and suggestive manner.

"Pass your line astern!" shouted Long John, "and you can tow him in."

Unshipping the rope from the notch, and quickly passing it astern, they soon had their captive hard and fast, with its mouth partly out of water, held by the chain alone.

"Now man the oars, boys, and pull slowly so not to drown him," said the doctor; and, with the thrashing, floundering creature as a rudder, they slowly pulled toward the breakwater, highly elated. It was such hard work that the dinghy was finally pressed into service, and after half an hour's rowing they reached the bridge that crossed the entrance to the outer moat. Here the boat was left, and, passing the line under the bridge, they took hold to haul the shark under, when the planks, old in the service, cracked, and down they went—boys, boards, and scantlings upon the shark. Tom and Harry clung to the planks, but Dick landed squarely on the shark. Such a thrashing around and getting out of the way was never seen before; but probably the shark was the most frightened of the party. The water was shallow, and amid much laughter and shouting they came out all right.

As the shark had now subsided, the line was passed to the tide-gate and along the wall, while

CATCHING A MAN-EATER. 227

two of the boys held some large boards as a slide. Finally, the word was given: the dozen or more colored men who had gathered around rushed away, and the shark went floundering over into its prison. It only remained to cut out the hook, and this delicate operation was performed by Long John. With a skillful cut of his blade the hook came out, and with a sav-

The pet shark.

age splash the man-eater dashed away amid the cheers of the lookers-on. Up the moat it swam, stirring up the mud, turning the corner at the second face; then, discovering that it was fairly caged, it assumed a more moderate rate of speed, and sailed up in plain view, much to the satisfaction of its captors.

"He must be twelve feet long," said Tom to his father.

"Easily that," replied the latter. "At least, as large as you would care to catch."

"Yes, indeed," Tom rejoined. "I don't care to try it again to-day; it's too hard work."

It was near sundown, and the boys returned to their quarters well pleased with the day's work.*

That evening the boys brought out all their hermit-crabs. They were in shells of all kinds. Some had gorgeous ones of dazzling pearl that had been partially cleaned with acid; others had taken up with top shells or a *Trochus*, while

---

* This shark was kept for six months, and was dubbed the Provost-Marshal by the dwellers in the fort. It steadily refused food, and probably died of starvation. Its jaw is now in the Museum of Natural History, Central Park, New York.

Diogenes of the old pipe lumbered about, creating a laugh at every move. The doctor pointed out to them the singular fact that the hermits, land and marine, were born in this defenseless condition, the abdomen or tail being soft, and that instinctively they sought out empty shells to live in; then he showed how nicely the big red or purple claws fitted into the opening of the shell, serving as an operculum.

The crabs were in constant warfare. Outgrowing their shells, they endeavored to oust their fellows, the stronger jerking out the weaker —a series of operations extremely interesting to the observers. Their hermits ranged from a gigantic marine form which they had found in a big strombus to the purple-clawed land-crabs common under the boards in the fort. When arranged in a group they looked like soldiers; indeed, soldier-crab was the name given them on the reef.

The doctor had encouraged the boys to collect all the animals found on the key, and they soon had an interesting list and a motley assemblage—cockroaches, scorpions, centipedes, mole-crickets, all of which must have been brought there by vessels, while many others had drifted in or were blown there by the wind. On all the keys a species of walking-stick was found. Scorpions lived on Loggerhead, and, according to Long John, a white variety. Many of the Northern and Southern birds stopped at the island during migration—cranes, curlews, and occasional flamingoes, flocks of butcher birds and numbers of beautiful fly-catchers, rail, gallinules, and one day the mangrove and cocoanut trees in the fort were the resting place for numerous cuckoos. Many of these birds were caught, and a tame gallinule, several rail, two or three pelicans and herons were added to the list of pets, while the rabbits— old Bon and Bess—they had brought from New

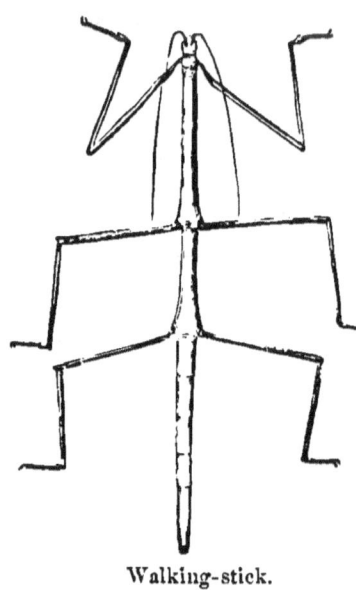

Walking-stick.

York had increased so from the original pair that they were taken to Loggerhead Key, where doubtless their descendants may still be found.

CHAPTER XIII.

A TURTLE TURN.

The expedition to Loggerhead Key—Another victim of the *Physalia*—A new pet added—Graining craw-fish—Tortoise-shell—Loggerhead light—Turning the turtle—Tom and Harry have a struggle—Almost carried overboard—Turned at last—The night's work.

"IT'S a-breezin' up from the east," said Long John one morning as the boys gathered on the wharf, "and turtle is layin'."

"A good time to try Loggerhead Key," suggested Tom.

"The very thing," responded Dick, while the others joined in and expressed their desire to visit the as yet unexplored key, famous for its large turtles and the sport their turning produced. Long John agreed that a better time could not be selected, so preparations for the start were at once commenced. The lines, a hamper of food, and fresh water were stowed in the dinghy which was towed behind the *Bull-pup*, and with a fair wind they stood out around the southwest channel, heading for the great needle-like tower that alike forms the land's end of the United States and the highest light-house in the country.

The key was about five miles distant, and, as there was good fishing on the way, Long John proposed that they should stop and catch a mess for supper. They found at the north end of Bird Key some large heads of coral, under which their bait appeared in the guise of craw-fishes. The grains soon brought them up flapping, and when enough had been caught they kept on toward a reef on the southwest channel.

"There's a friend of yours, Tom," said Harry, as a large Portuguese man-o'-war appeared.

"Yes," replied Tom, standing up and holding on to the shrouds; "I know all about him.

But what is that under him? A turtle, surely. Luff a little, please."

Long John hauled the boat up in the wind a trifle, and seizing a large scoop-net, Tom lowered it under the *Physalia* and drew it up, and with it a turtle about a foot long that had been

Craw-fish.

overpowered by its violent stinging apparatus. Tom rubbed the purple mass away and finally anointed the animal with oil amid the laughter of the rest. Tom was a humanitarian. The turtle was a hawk's-bill, the kind so valued for its shell in trade.

"It is too bad to lose this breeze by stopping to fish," said the doctor finally. "Suppose we keep on and haul the seine at Loggerhead instead."

This plan was received with favor, so Long John kept the boat away from the point where he intended anchoring, and they sped along down the channel at a famous pace, making the dinghy jump around, much to the discomfort of Long John's dog, "Sugar," that was endeavoring to take a nap in it. They gradually neared the key, and finally made soundings about a quarter of a mile out. The water was too rough to see the bottom distinctly, but it was covered with a rich growth of fans, plumes, and small head corals that suddenly came to an end fifty yards from the beach in a circle of pure white sand seemingly made for the bather. The sail was now lowered and a few moments later the anchor was dropped. Taking the dinghy, the party pulled ashore, hauling the boat well beyond tide-water upon the sand.

Nearly opposite the big tower they came to a path which led to a commodious house for such an isolated spot, occupied by the light-house keeper and his family, who gave them a cordial welcome. After some refreshments the party started off to examine the key and the big light.

The island was almost entirely covered with bay-cedar bushes, with here and there patches of cactus. Its inhabitants were gulls, hermit and spirit crabs, and a few insects. In pushing through the brush Dick noticed a curious stick on his coat, and, in brushing it off, discovered that it was alive.

"It's a walking-stick," said the doctor, laughing at the surprise of the boys, who had never seen the insect before, "and one of the most remarkable of all the mimics. In the extreme tropics there is one nearly a foot long. The walking-leaves are equally curious," added the doctor, "being so almost exact in their resemblance that they find absolute protection in it."

The brush grew thick and it was hot and close; but the boys found something to amuse them at almost every step. Big hermit-crabs were plentiful, and a large purple land-crab was exceedingly common, sulking under the cactus or climbing upon the low branches of the bay-cedar. As they came out upon the beach the spirit-crabs dashed in every direction. They were as white as the sand itself, and their name well suited them, as they appeared and disappeared in a most ghostly manner. They were continually tempting the boys to a race, and it was very difficult to catch them, as they scurried about this way and that, most successful dodgers. They only took to the water when closely pressed, and then with great reluctance, coming out immediately, lifting their long colorless stalked eyes as if to see if the persecution was to be continued. The beach was tunneled everywhere with their holes, showing that they were successful and experienced miners. After a stroll along the beach, picking up shells, sponges, and fans, the boys returned to the anchorage, where Long John had built a fire, upon which some mullets were giving out savory odors.

"You've seen floating coral and brain coral, but here's pepper coral," said Long John, handing Tom a piece of coral with very fine pores or cells.

"Why do you call it pepper coral?" asked Tom.

"Taste it," was the fisherman's reply.

Nothing daunted, Tom bit off a portion, and a moment later, concealing his emotion and the tears that stood in his eyes, he handed the coral to Dick, who also fell into the trap.

The coral bit the tongue even more than pepper, the smarting sensation lasting some time, and the boys agreed that it was well named and almost as disagreeable as the prickly pear which Harry had essayed to eat without removing the skin, filling his lips with the minute barbs.

The boys had ridden big turtles and were familiar with them, but they had never spent a night on the beach watching for them, and when supper was over they stretched themselves on the sand to receive their instructions from Long John, who was an old turtle-turner.

"Turtles ain't particularly smart," he began, "but they're cunning, and you have got to go for 'em jest so. Now, they don't come up till the moon's risen; then they come in shore, look around, and, if it's all right and quiet like, they come up. If it isn't, they don't; so you want to lay low. When they make up their minds to come in, they don't waste any time, but come right up, dig the hole, lay their eggs, cover 'em up, and go back down another track. Now, we want to divide up into parties of two or three and get stations all along the beach about three hundred yards apart. Sit close in by the bush, and every few minutes some one must run down to the water edge and walk along to the next station, and in this way cover all the beach. When you see a track, jest sing out, follow it up on the run, and grab the turtle by the side, then turn her if you kin," he added, with the grin that he seemed to manufacture only on special occasions.

The boys laid around on the beach until the moon came up, enjoying the beautiful evening and listening to the gulls, then took stations as Long John had directed, and began the patrol. It was a perfectly quiet night, even the musical rill of the water upon the sands being low and sweet. From the outer reef came a faint moaning of the surf, and occasionally the cry of a stray laughing gull was heard.

Tom and Dick were lying together flat upon the sands, looking up at the stars, the doctor and Harry having taken their station to the south, when there came a low but distinct hiss. Tom impulsively started up with an exclamation, but Dick pulled him back. Again came the hiss, and then in the silvery path of the moon a black head glistened on the water. A moment later a black body was seen clambering slowly over the sands not fifty feet below them.

"It's a turtle," whispered Tom, starting up again.

"But suppose it isn't," retorted Dick; "suppose it is something else."

"Well, what?" asked Tom impatiently.

"I don't know," was the reply.

"It's a turtle fast enough," said Tom. "Let's wait until it gets well up, then we will rush at it."

They remained perfectly quiet, and in a few minutes the turtle was high on the beach near the line of brush, evidently making the sand fly.

"Now," said Tom, "let's sneak up until it sees us, then hail the rest."

Accordingly, they crept along on their hands and knees for a few feet, when suddenly a long sigh or snort was heard, and the big turtle was seen making for the water. At this the boys uttered loud shouts and rushed ahead. Tom reached the animal first, and, seizing it by the shell, lifted with all his strength. To his surprise, he received a heavy blow in the face from the big fore flipper that was whirling like a windmill. Down went the animal again, pulling Harry head-foremost to the sand, while Tom swung around on its back and tried to hold it back. The turtle could easily carry both of them, and soon tripped him up.

"Let's both try this side," cried Tom; so both took hold of the same side, and, dodging the flying flippers, lifted with all their strength. "Up she comes! now, all together!"

The boys lifted with a will, but the moment the big flipper was clear of the ground it struck

Dick such a sounding blow that he let go, and the big reptile pulled Tom to his knees again.

"He'll get away from us sure," exclaimed the latter, clinging desperately to the side of the shell, but being carried down the beach. "Help!" he shouted. "We've got him, but we can't keep him."

"There's a plank," cried Tom; "try that."

Dick seized the plank that had been washed ashore, and, thrusting it beneath the turtle, tried to use it as a lever, while Tom stood in front and tried to intimidate the turtle that was bent upon reaching the water. She would have escaped had not the doctor and Harry arrived from one direction, while Long John and the keeper's son came running from the other.

"Now then, again," shouted Tom, hopefully. "Up she goes! Heave o'!"

Three or four pairs of arms grasped the monster this time and over she went, flapping her bright-yellow breast with powerful strokes.

"Well done," said Long John. "I'd reckoned that she would pull you into the water."

"So she would," replied Tom, puffing and

breathing hard. "We never could have stopped her if you hadn't come up."

Long John cut a slit in the turtle's flippers, making them fast with rope yarn, and then the party separated again.

In the course of the night five large loggerhead turtles were caught, and by three o'clock the young turtle-turners were well tired out.

The next day their prisoners were placed in the large boat and taken over to the fort, where they were released in the turtle crawl.

Star-fish.

CHAPTER XIV.

THE PET-HOUSE.

Some remarkable pets—Young turtles—Bon, the goat—Bess and Jack—The pet-house—The gulls, pelicans, and crabs—The tame gopher, chickens, and pigeons—The little turtles—Growth of coral.

ONE of the turtles had succeeded in laying forty or fifty eggs before it was caught at Loggerhead Key, and these Long John had brought home, giving some to the boys and eating the rest. Tom buried his in the sand in an inclosure, and was rewarded in time with a dozen young loggerhead turtles that afforded no little amusement, and soon became interesting pets.

The instinct of these little creatures was remarkable, as the boys tested on many occasions. When placed on the floor of the little office, they invariably crawled in the direction of the door which led into the water. How these helpless turtle infants knew the water was there puzzled

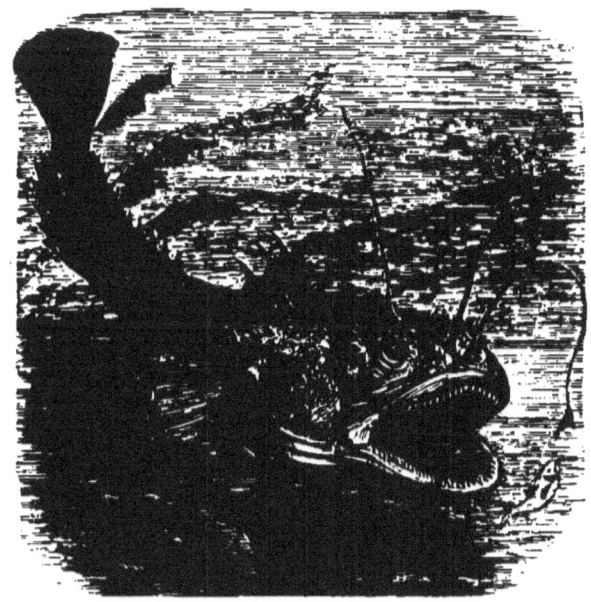

The lophius.

the boys. When Tom would open the door they would crawl toward it, tumble into the water, and go paddling off.

The time was not all passed upon the water, though nearly every day an excursion of some kind was made. The weather was so warm that they often went in bathing several times during the day, diving from the dock, and under the tutelage of Paublo becoming expert swimmers. The fishing even from the wharf was good, snappers, grunts, and the barracuda being caught here, while from the upper wharf they often captured a beautiful *Cyprœa*—the shell climbing up the teredo-eaten piles, from which they were taken by the skillful young divers. Often they would lie on the timbers of the wharf for hours, watching the wonderful variety of fish-life, observing their curious ways and habits, their games and antics.

The aquarium was a favorite spot. The little office had been fitted up by the doctor, and here were their microscopes, their collecting-jars, instruments, and everything appertaining to the study. Here they could sit and look out of the open door into the aquarium and watch the movements of the various animals they had placed there. From the walk that surrounded the basin they could see the anemones, star-fish, trepangs, craw-fish, the sly octopus crawling over the dead coral rock, or the agile squid as it darted here and there, the gar-fish that never or rarely left the surface, and the curious fishing-frog, or *Lophius*, with its fishing-rod, that as closely clung to the bottom.

The doctor had placed specimens of all kinds

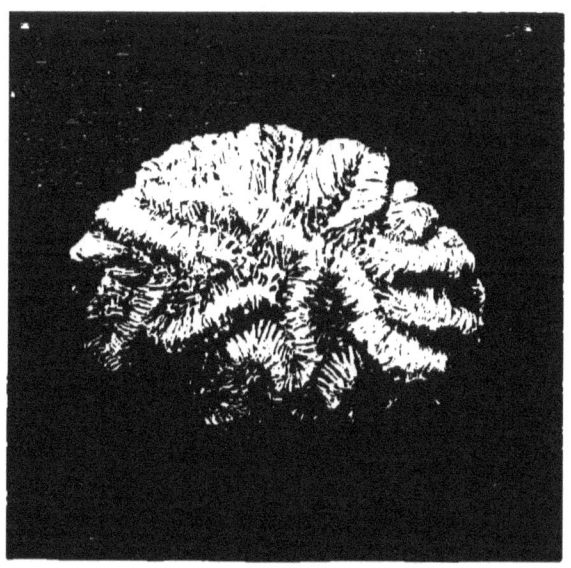

Meandrina convexa. Tortugas, Florida, growth of which was watched by Dr. J. B. Holder.

of coral found on the reef in the inclosure, watching them from day to day to determine the rapidity of their growth, and many facts new to science were discovered. He found that coral grew much more rapidly than was formerly supposed. A common brick, upon which the accompanying head of *Mœandrina* had fastened itself, was closely observed, and as a result its growth was estimated at one inch per year. The branch-corals grew at least six or eight inches a year—observations that were new and interesting.

As the weeks passed on, the collections constantly accumulated, and, when opportunity offered, many treasures were sent North to the Cambridge Museum, the Smithsonian Institution, and the College of the City of New York, while various schools and friends were supplied with sets of corals and shells. The fishes were shipped in alcohol, with many of the smaller and more delicate animals, as the anemones, star-fishes, sea-pigeons, while the gorgonias or sea-fans were carefully dried. The corals were bleached by allowing them to stand for a week in stale water, when they were thoroughly rinsed and syringed with fresh water, to remove every portion of the animal. Then the branches were placed in the sun, soon bleaching a pure white.

THE PET-HOUSE. 249

When ready for shipment they were packed in barrels and boxes in shavings or bay-cedar leaves as the case might be.

A group of sea birds.

Many evenings were passed in the little room that soon became a home for the boys, and where the doctor talked to them about their finds and explained many of the mysteries of the deep sea, always finding in these wonders new evidences of a higher wisdom which was impressed upon his hearers.

The pets accumulated day by day, as all the boys were fond of animals. Tom had two tame porcupine-fishes that swam through his fingers, while the turtle that was rescued from the *Physalia* was tied to a stake by a hole in its shell, and considered a pet, though it must be confessed it showed little evidence of domestication. Tame gulls and noddies stalked about, keeping Dick busy in providing them with food, while Harry, having reared two young pelicans, which he took from a rude nest on Bush Key, was similarly employed in supplying them with fishes. Long John had made him a small cast-net, and with this and a long iron barrel-hoop with which, by using it as a saber, he cut down sardines, he provided for these pets that were always hungry and never satisfied.

The crab in the pipe-bowl was an especial

pet of the doctor, the clanging of its home being heard at all hours. Other pets were a gorgeous purple gallinule and several rails that were blown ashore in a gale of wind, while a pet goat— "Bon"—a white heron, and a sooty tern shared the affections of the whole party.

The pets increased so in numbers that finally the doctor had a large inclosure made out from the boatswain's quarters, in which various pets were kept, affording much amusement and delight to their youthful owners.

Not a day passed but something occurred to form the topic of interesting conversation. Sudden squalls or storms would drive strange birds ashore, while the following day the beaches would be strewed with shells and the flotsam and jetsam of the gulf.

One day Tom heard cries of a gull in distress, and was witness to one of the contests of Nature. A wily laughing-gull had alighted on Long John's pelican and, quickly snatching the fish from its bill, soared aloft with cries of delight; but before it could make way with the prize a man-o'-war bird—another thief—heard the outcry and darted forth. Then began a chase that was magnificent in its evolutions. The gull sought to rise, but the swift man-o'-war bird dashed after it, rising higher and higher, and finally shot by. It turned, hesitated a moment, then projected itself like a meteor at the gull. The latter, with wild cries, attempted to avoid it, and then in despair dropped the fish, which the man-o'-war bird had followed, catching it before it struck the water, bearing it off in triumph.

Many nights were spent on the water listening to the tales of Long John or old Busby, while Chief and Bob Rand, who were upon rare occasions tempted out by the enthusiasm of the boys, would sit and listen, but seldom say a word. Sometimes a smack would come in with its well loaded with groupers, yellow-tails, and porgies, bound for the Havana market, or the fleet schooner *Tortugas* would go over and bring them back guava jelly and various dainties. In this way the happy days passed in this land of perpetual summer. As their acquaintance with their pets increased, their peculiar traits developed. The two rabbits which the doctor had brought from New York afforded never-ending amusement. They had little pens to themselves, with stairs leading up to little rooms and a second story—an arrangement that was very necessary in the case of old Jack, a handsome lop-eared black and white rabbit. He was so ferocious that he enjoyed being attacked, and, far from running away, would chase the boys at every opportunity. Sometimes he was taken up into the fort and placed in the yard about the little cottage where the boys lived. Playing that Jack was a bull, they would imitate the Spanish bull-fight, dashing into the yard and out again very rapidly with Jack at their heels. Occasionally they failed to make good their escape, and his sharp teeth and claws would rend their clothes wherever he could seize them.

Bon, the goat, was most esteemed. She provided them with all the milk for their coffee, and was harnessed up at times to drive around the fort. When released, she had a trick of running at a perpendicular wall, planting her feet against it, then leaping off, landing upon her feet again, this singular performance being repeated time and again before the lookers-on. The pigeons Tom trained so that they would alight upon his head and shoulders when he entered the yard, while even the chickens were educated, to the astonishment of the boatswain, who one day, when he saw one of the old gopher turtles walking slowly off with a cat upon its back, raised his hands and announced that "them boys took the constraint out of onything he'd ever seen."

The pet-house was so arranged that the water came into the yard at high tide, when ducks, geese, gulls, pelicans, cranes, rail, and the purple gallinule waded, picking up the shrimps, worms, and other animals that came out, and presenting at such times a singular scene.

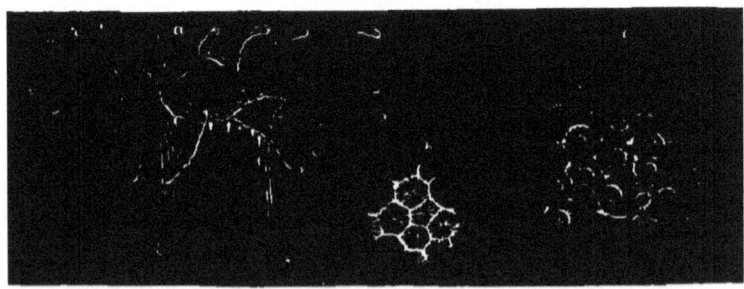

Dana's astrangia (*Astrangia Danæ*, Agassiz): *c*, a growing cluster; *a*, a single polyp enlarged; *b*, the dead coral.

CHAPTER XV.

HAULING THE SEINE.

Attacked by a sting-ray—The nurse shark—Gambols beneath the water—Tameness of fishes—Angel-fishes—Hauling the seine by moonlight—The mangrove-root city—A wonderful catch—A shark in the toils.

TURTLE and egg time had passed, yet the naturalists lingered on the reef. The days continued the same clear sunny ones they had experienced all summer, the blue waters of the gulf often for many hours being as smooth as glass, with not a ripple save where some leaping barracuda or hungry pelican disturbed the surface. These days were spent by the party in deep-water collecting, the boat being sculled slowly along just outside the great barrier-reef, or toward the old wreck to the south, in water thirty or forty feet deep, and so clear that every object upon the bottom could be distinctly seen. The reef here was devoid of branch coral, the bottom being covered with a short-leaved variety.

Eager faces peered over the gunwale as the boat drifted along, and the moment a shell or a bunch of rare coral appeared, two or three ardent collectors would plunge over and race to the bottom to secure the prize.

On one occasion Dick was poling the boat along, while Harry sat in the bow astride the cut-water, with a bare leg hanging overboard on either side. The water was shallow, and it seemed the last place to expect an enemy; but suddenly a big black sting-ray started up, and Harry gave a cry of pain and rolled back into the boat, while the bird-like form dashed away. He had been struck across the top of his foot in three parallel lines by the sharp stings of the whip-ray, leaving jagged and painful wounds.

Following up the animal, they speared it, and the bony serrated spine is still in Tom's possession. The tail of the sting-ray resembled the lash of a whip, the stings being just at the base of the tail, one above the other. Just how the wound was made the boys could not conjecture.

During one of their submarine excursions a sleeping nurse was started up, its black form creating a momentary panic among the divers. Planting their feet against the bottom, they thrust themselves up to the surface as quickly as possible.

As seen from the boat, the white forms scrambling about, fifteen or twenty feet below, presented an amusing spectacle. The boys could see each other very distinctly beneath the water, even a submarine smile or wink being readily detected. Sometimes their jokes resulted in making the boys laugh outright, thus taking in mouthfuls of water and bringing about a general rush to the surface.

In these submarine excursions they often noticed a peculiarity that is familiar in the atmosphere. In diving twenty or more feet, strata of different temperatures would be encountered. At the surface the water would be very warm for ten or twelve feet; then the swimmer would enter a cold stratum, and going deeper would reach a warmer area, and emerging again from

Decorating in captivity.

the warm area would at the very bottom enter into one colder than all. Even in swimming on the surface, cold and warm rivers, so to speak, were often met with.

While swimming, many fishes were disposed to examine the boys from mere curiosity, as if they wondered what kind of an animal this was that had so suddenly appeared upon their mountain home; for we must remember that the marine inhabitants also have hills, valleys, and mountains, and the dwellers on the reef were highlanders, living far above those in the water a mile away, and under pressures differing as the air pressures differ between high mountains and valleys on land.

One afternoon the boys had been on a trip down the reef, and were returning by Bush Key, when Harry suddenly stood up and pointed to a collection of submerged roots that were strewed about. "Look at the angel-fishes!" he exclaimed; and, dropping the oars, the others also stood up and saw the most wonderful assemblage of these beautiful creatures they had yet observed.

The roots were those of the mangrove trees that had been washed out into the lagoon between Bush and Long Keys, and in three or four feet of water their tangled masses formed excellent homes for innumerable and resplendent small fry. When the boat was pushed nearer, the great black roots were seen to fairly blossom with these animated flowers. Some were yellow, blue, and brown, with eyes of beautiful hues, and others, not angel-fishes, were of a most intense blue. All moved about with great deliberation, and flashed here and there like living gems.

"If we only had the seine!" whispered Harry, as if fearful of disturbing the living panorama before them.

"Why not go and get it?" suggested Tom.

"My proposition," said the doctor, "is that we come out to-night and haul the seine by moonlight."

This being decided upon, the oars were resumed, and the boat went rushing through the water toward the fort, accompanied by the pet pelican that had espied them from afar and joined them, expecting its supper. It was always hungry.

The nights on the reef were often almost

counterparts of the days, and as the party pushed off after supper, carrying the seine piled in a great heap in the bow, and with collecting-cans stowed in between the seats, the moon was just rising over Bush Key, casting a flood of radiance over the lagoon, and lighting up the sands of Long Key until they gleamed like silver. Not a sound could be heard save the creaking of the oars and their monotonous clink in the rowlocks, or an occasional splash from the outer reef, followed by a thundering crash, telling of some huge fish that had essayed to leave its native element and had fallen heavily back in obedience to the law of gravity.

The pull to Bush Key was a short one, and soon the boat rounded to near the mangrove roots.

"Now, boys," said the doctor, "we must work carefully. Don't rush in too quickly, or you will tear the net. Two of you take the end and run it out; and when it is stretched we will all move toward Bush Key beach, some of you tossing out the roots."

These orders were followed literally. Tom and Dick leaped overboard, the water being about three feet deep, and taking an end stick of the seine, walked or waded away with it, while the others payed it out regularly. They made a long sweep, so as to surround the roots, and, when two thirds of the net had been hauled over, Harry and Long John went overboard and drew the other end of the seine toward shore— the net now presenting a semicircle. The doctor now pushed the dinghy just inside the bend of the net and gave signal to go ahead.

What a sight it was! The moon was looking over the mangroves on the keys, bathing the fishermen in its light. The net came slowly in; the doctor or Long John called a halt whenever a root was found, these obstructions being lifted and the occupants frightened out of the home that was then tossed outside of the floats; then the signal would be again given, and the seine taken in until another root was met, and so on for half an hour or more, when, the ground being clear, the net went rapidly in.

"Look at them!" cried Tom, who was haul-

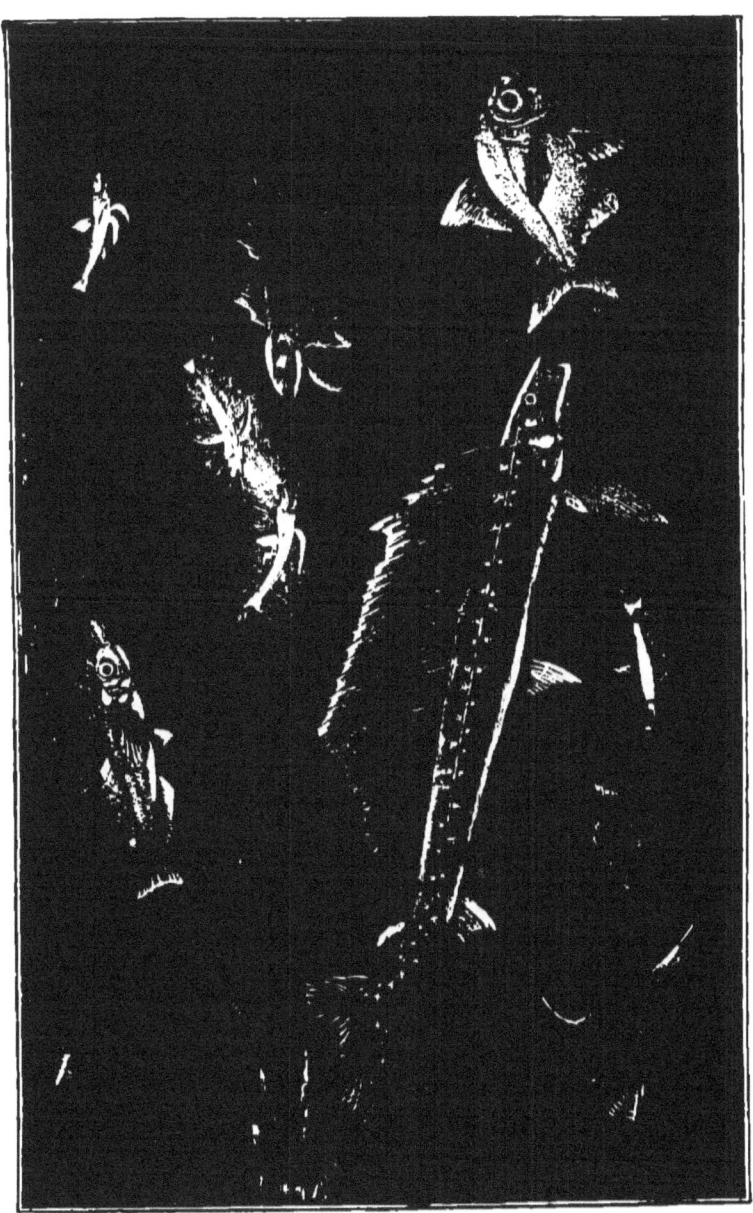

Luminous fish of the deep sea.

ing at the end; "angels, snappers, grunts, and—there's a shark, too!" Sure enough, a small shark was in the toils, making the water boil and demoralizing the other prisoners, who made desperate efforts to escape from his struggles. This would not do, and, seizing a boat-hook, Long John waded in and soon had the young man-eater in the toils. He seemed to be about three feet and a half long. Long John lifted him over to the beach, where he soon flopped back into the water and escaped.

The net was now well in shore, and the splashing and beating of innumerable fish commenced. One more pull, and the finny assemblage was in shallow water. The sight of their catch soon exhausted the adjectives of even the young enthusiasts. There were hundreds and thousands of fishes, leaping, splashing, and bounding, one over another: angel-fishes in gorgeous tints, brown-hued snappers dripping with the molten gold of phosphorescence, yellow grunts making audible protest, ugly toad-fish, long gar-fish, rakish barracuda, prickly porcupine-fish inflating their balloon-like bodies. Over all, creating a noise like falling rain, flapped countless mullets with sides gleaming like silver. Besides these, there were craw-fishes, echini, starfishes, crabs, and an occasional octopus; in fact, almost every animal to be found on the great reef was represented in these mangrove-root communities.

"Now, boys," said the doctor, when their excitement had somewhat abated, "hold the net steady, and remember our rule—not to kill more than we can actually use."

The seine was well up, but the fish were still massed in enough water to keep them alive, and out of this wonderful collection the young naturalists made their selection. Of grunts, snappers, and the commoner fishes they had long ago secured a good supply, and only the rare forms were taken, together with some small specimens which the doctor thought might be new to science. The net was then raised and the affrighted throng released, to swim back again to the old roots and perhaps exchange opinions as to the cause of their remarkable experience.

It was a merry party that pulled back over the lagoon that night, and as they turned into bed they little dreamed what the following day would develop.

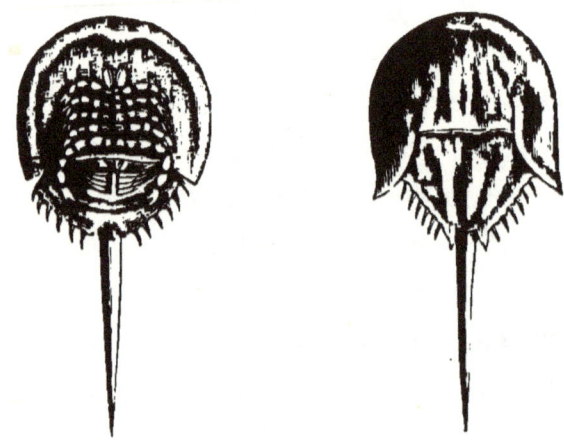

Horseshoe-crab.

CHAPTER XVI.

THE HURRICANE.

The boatswain's warning—Securing the boats—The hurricane—Busby pronounces the house unsafe—The fall of the building—Work of the hurricane on the reef—The *Rosetta* and *Tortugas* wrecked—Departure for the North—Last days on the reef—The results.

EARLY the next morning Tom was aroused by some one standing in the doorway, and, raising up, he saw that it was the old boatswain with his famous spy-glass under his arm.

"I've jest been down to the boat-house making things snug," he said, "and Bob wanted me to ask you if you wouldn't give him a haul with the *Bull-pup*."

"What is the matter?" asked Tom.

"It's goin' to blow, and blow hard," replied the old sailor.

"But it's as clear as clear can be," said Tom, getting up and looking out of the window.

"Well," rejoined Busby, "I tuk a gaze aboot with her," tapping the glass, "and I've concluded its goin' to blow, and blow hard; and so has Bob, and John, and Chief. Don't you hear that?" he asked, putting his hand to his ear.

The boys listened silently, and from far away there seemed to come a faint moan. Ten minutes later Tom, who had run to the top of the fort, saw a dark cloud over beyond Loggerhead that had an ominous appearance. "The barometer is going down as if the bottom had fallen out," announced Harry, who had been out to examine it. "I guess we are in for it."

The boys hurried down to the dock to lend a hand with the rest in pulling the old *Bull-pup* on the ways eight or ten feet above high-water mark. They then looked around to see if everything else was snug. They were none too soon, for a short time after a squall struck the key, gradually increasing in strength during the day, the shrieking and howling of the wind and the roar of the waters keeping every one awake nearly all the night. The following morning it was blowing a hurricane, and as the boys struggled up on the fort and looked out from behind the grim battlements a fearful scene was presented. The water, so smooth two nights previous, was now covered by a mass of foam that, caught by the wind, was carried high into the air. The sea appeared to be making a clean breach over Bush and Long Keys; many of the trees had disappeared, while the lower portion of Long Key was washed away. The wind was so powerful that they could scarcely show their heads above the wall. Sticks, gravel, and all movable objects were flying through the air like hailstones. The cocoa-nut trees had been despoiled of their beauty; their leaves had been beaten into shapeless whips, and from many the foliage was entirely twisted off.

Later, Tom, who was looking out of the window, cried out, "Here comes the boatswain!" And, sure enough, the old sailor was seen, bent double, buffeted by the gusts, enveloped in a whirlwind of sand, and headed toward the house. As he reached the fence he grasped it and held on, beckoning with his arm. As Tom stepped out to meet him the old man shouted: "You'd better come out o' that, all hands!"

"What for?" screamed Tom.

"It's a-gittin' worse. I never see the like," again shouted Busby, crawling up the steps, "and I don't like the look o' *that*," pointing to the big four-storied brick building that, only partly finished, stood near, towering high above the cottage next to that occupied by the party.

"What were you saying?" asked the doctor, who now appeared, and as the boatswain repeated the warning he said to the boys around him: "I hardly think there is any danger myself, but it is always best to take the advice of those who know more about such things than we do, so we will leave the cottage."

Accordingly, a short time after the little party were struggling toward the casemates. The wind had increased to a frightful degree, and as they reached a clearing midway between the cottage and the arches they had to crouch low to avoid being blown over. As they pressed on, a frightful gust came, and then for an instant a strange lull was felt. At an exclamation from Busby they all turned, and saw, to their horror, the huge walls of the brick building rocking and trembling; then, with a wild roar and an appalling crash, the mass of stone, mortar, brick, and broken beams went down before the hurricane, crushing like pasteboard the cottage next to theirs. From the ruins for a second rose a great white cloud of dust that whirled about like a living thing and was borne away on the gale.

The boys, who were often in the crushed house, were too thankful at their escape to say a word; indeed, amid the roar they could only look their gratitude at the boatswain, who, always cheerful, responded by sundry winks and nods, as much as to say: "I told you so!"

This hurricane did great damage on all the keys, and in the West Indies generally. It continued all the afternoon, and not until the next morning did the end come, and not until then did the young naturalists venture out. Their own quarters were safe, had escaped the falling building by a miracle; but outside there was a scene of ruin. The sea had encroached upon the island, beaten down one of the docks, partly washed away the aquarium, and hurled coral-rock in a confused mass upon the beach. Amid the wreckage Tom found a small board bearing the name "Rosetta" in copper letters, and, hauling it out, eyed it with sorrow and regret. It was all that was left of the boat that had carried them so many times over the reef.

She had been torn from her place during the extreme high water and literally ground to pieces, the stern-board being all that was left.

The hurricane caused great devastation in Key West. Its force may be understood from this incident: A vessel lying near Havana was blown without sails across to Key West in an incredibly short time, the crew finding themselves in the morning high and dry on Key West beach. The city was flooded; vessels were sunk at the wharf, and among them the schooner *Tortugas*, that had borne the young naturalists on many a trip.

These and other events resulted in the departure of the party for the North; not without regret, as the months passed here had been of the greatest interest and value. For the doctor and Tom it was but a partial breaking up, as they returned to the little garden in the gulf and remained for several years.

The old boatman lies by the deep sea on the Florida Reef.

www.ingramcontent.com/pod-product-compliance
Lightning Source LLC
Chambersburg PA
CBHW032113230426
43672CB00009B/1726